Beyond the Makerspace

SWEETLAND DIGITAL RHETORIC COLLABORATIVE

Series Editors:
Anne Ruggles Gere, University of Michigan
Naomi Silver, University of Michigan

The Sweetland Digital Rhetoric Collaborative Book Series publishes texts that investigate the multiliteracies of digitally mediated spaces both within academia as well as other contexts.

DIGITALCULTUREBOOKS, an imprint of the University of Michigan Press, is dedicated to publishing work in new media

Beyond the Makerspace

Making and Relational Rhetorics

ANN SHIVERS-MCNAIR

UNIVERSITY OF MICHIGAN PRESS

ANN ARBOR

Published in the United States of America by the
University of Michigan Press
Printed and bound by CPI Group (UK) Ltd, Croydon, CR0 4YY

First published June 2021

A CIP catalog record for this book is available from the British Library.

Library of Congress Cataloging-in-Publication data has been applied for.

ISBN 978-0-472-05485-5 (paper: alk. paper)
ISBN 978-0-472-90241-5 (ebook OA)
Library of Congress Control Number: 2021935578
https://doi.org/10.3998/mpub.11724511

The publisher gratefully acknowledges the support of the Sweetland Center for
Writing in making this book possible.

Contents

Digital materials related to this title can be found on the Fulcrum platform via the following citable URL: https://doi.org/10.3998/mpub.11724511

Acknowledgments

I am grateful to all the people who participated in this project—especially Tony Loiseleur, Clarissa San Diego, Eric Renn, Richard Albritton, Alex Cheker, and Micah Summers—for generously welcoming me into their spaces and processes, for transforming how I think about and do both making and writing, and for being comakers of the knowledge in this book. Eric welcomed me into SoDo Makerspace in February 2015, and thus began this project. Tony and Clarissa read and provided helpful feedback on versions of this book, and Tony made and gave me the 3D-printed spatial manipulation toy featured on the cover of the book and in Chapter 3. I am also grateful to my former University of Washington students in two sections of English 382, Rhetoric in the Making, for their creativity and insights that have transformed how I teach and think about making.

For their invaluable guidance and feedback, I would like to thank the editors who helped me shape this and earlier versions of portions of this work. I thank Matthew Vetter and Kristi McDuffie, editors for a 2017 *Kairos* webtext in which a portion of Chapter 2 appears; Anna Smith and Paul Prior, editors of a 2020 special issue of *Learning, Culture, and Social Interaction* in which a portion of Chapter 4 appears; and Huatong Sun and Guiseppe Getto, editors of a 2017 special issue of *Technical Communication* in which a portion of Chapter 5 appears. I am profoundly grateful to the editorial team, board, and three anonymous readers at the University of Michigan Sweetland Digital Rhetoric Collaborative for their feedback on and support of this project, and especially to Anne Gere and Naomi Silver for recognizing potential in my work and for supporting me as I developed and revised this book. I am equally grateful to the editorial team at the

University of Michigan Press, especially Sara Cohen, Mary Hashman, and Flannery Wise, for expertly guiding and supporting me through the final revisions and production process.

This project would not have been possible without the intellectual, material, and emotional support of colleagues and mentors. I am grateful to the College of Social and Behavioral Sciences and the English Department at the University of Arizona for research funding and time that sustained my fieldwork and writing, and I am grateful to my University of Arizona colleagues for their friendship, encouragement, and support as I worked on this project. I especially thank Sallie Koenig for her help with proofreading and indexing. I am also grateful to the University of Washington English Department for a dissertation fellowship that supported earlier fieldwork for this book. I owe a special thanks to Joyce Inman, who mentored me into rhetoric and composition and encouraged me along the way. And I owe a debt of gratitude to mentors across institutions—especially Adela Licona, Angela Haas, Natasha Jones, Michelle Eble, and Rebecca Walton—who generously mentor me in addition to their own colleagues and students, and whose work to center marginalized bodies and traditions continually inspires and instructs me.

I am immensely grateful to Anis Bawarshi, Juan Guerra, Candice Rai, and Mark Zachry for their guidance and support as I developed this project, for their example of the kind of scholar I aspire to be, and for their friendship. Anis, my dissertation director, believed in me and in this project from the beginning, and he read many versions and gave generative feedback that shaped my work in and beyond this book. I am also grateful beyond words to Laura Gonzales, without whom this book would not have come to be, and whose brilliance, generosity, courage, and example have made this project and everything I do better.

Finally, I am thankful to my family for believing in me, for supporting me, and for bearing with me. I am thankful to my Seattle family, Diane, Juan, Amy, and Anis, for caring for me throughout this project and especially when I was far away from my spouse and the rest of my family. I am thankful to my academic friends-turned-family, Laura and Victor, for their love, generosity, and wisdom. I am thankful to my parents, Beth and Jerry, for a lifetime of love and encouragement. And I am thankful to my spouse, Daniel, for his love and intellectual partnership, and for creating the beautiful image on the cover of this book.

- A portion of Chapter 2 was first published in Ann Shivers-McNair, "3D Interviewing with Researcher POV Video: Bodies and Knowledge in the Making," *Kairos: Rhetoric, Technology, and Pedagogy* 21(2) (2017), http://praxis.technorhetoric.net/tiki-index.php?page=Praxis Wiki%3A_%3A3D+Interviewing. A portion of Chapter 4 was first published in Ann Shivers-McNair, "Mediation and Boundary Marking: A Case Study of Making Literacies in a Makerspace," *Learning, Culture, and Social Interaction* 20 (2020): 1–7, and is reprinted with permission from Elsevier. A portion of Chapter 5 was first published in Ann Shivers-McNair and Clarissa San Diego, "Localizing Communities, Goals, Communication, and Inclusion: A Collaborative Approach," *Technical Communication* 64(2) (2017): 97–112, and is reprinted with permission from the Society for Technical Communication.

Introduction

Making

Making is not new, but it is having a moment. That moment is the global maker movement that arose at the turn of the millennium. The beginnings of the contemporary movement are often associated with the first publication of *Make: Magazine* in 2005 by the entity now known as Make Community LLC and formerly known as Maker Media Inc., an investor-funded company that went out of business in June 2019 and was reconstituted as a member-funded organization in July 2019 (Dougherty 2019). Attendance at maker faires, Make Community–branded conventions featuring local makers, increased from 22,000 in 2006 to more than 1.4 million in more than two hundred cities worldwide in 2016 (Maker Media 2017). Many more cities across the world are home to makerspaces, which are workshops that offer access to and training on fabrication technologies like 3D printers and laser cutters, often with a focus on education and entrepreneurship. In the United States, President Barack Obama highlighted the maker movement when the White House hosted a maker faire in 2014 and a National Week of Making in 2015.

In other words, by 2014, the contemporary maker movement was well established, and multiple makerspaces had materialized (and dematerialized) in Seattle, where I lived at the time. But "makerspace" was a new word for me when I heard it in a conversation at an academic conference in October 2014, and I used my phone to surreptitiously search the web for a definition because it seemed like a word I should already know. Later that same evening, I searched the web again, this time for "Seattle makerspace," because I wanted to know if I could find one near me. The first promising result from my Google search was SoDo Makerspace, located in Seattle's South of Downtown (SoDo) neighborhood. I was intrigued, but also intimidated. After all, I had only just learned a word that many other people seemed to already know, and I had no background in engineering or design. For most of my life, I had thought of myself as a writer—it was always my focus in academic work, and all my jobs after graduating from college had been about writing. How would a writer fit into a makerspace?

I finally visited SoDo Makerspace a few months later, in February 2015. I arrived on a Saturday for an open tour advertised on the website. When I arrived and met Eric Renn, the founder and CEO of the makerspace, I was caught off guard by his first question: "So, what do you want to make?" I couldn't answer the question, because I had no idea what I could make. I left the tour dazzled by all the machines and objects I'd seen, and I was especially preoccupied with Eric's question. Despite my struggle to answer it in the context of an unfamiliar space with intimidating machines, that question—*What do you want to make?*—resonates with questions that writers, writing teachers, and writing researchers have been asking for a long time.

I began this book project in an attempt to answer Eric's question, along with my own questions about making, the maker movement, and makerspaces. In 2015, I set out to conduct a longitudinal, ethnographically informed case study of a Seattle makerspace in order to gain a rich understanding of a local instance of this global phenomenon. I wanted to understand what (and whose) values and practices we are taking up and what boundaries we mark when we identify as makers or when we turn a writing classroom or a library space into a makerspace. The boundaries of what counts as "writing" and who counts as "writer"—particularly in relation to what counts as "making" and who counts as "maker"—have long been the concern of scholars across several areas of rhetoric and writing studies, including cultural and feminist rhetorics, material rhetorics, digital rhetorics, multimodal composition, and professional and technical communication. These areas come from different epistemologies and theoretical traditions, but they share a recognition that boundaries between discursive and material (and between human and nonhuman) are negotiated and marked, rather than given.

This book takes up these conversations and focuses on relations and boundary-marking practices in acts of making—especially what counts as making and who counts as a maker. These boundaries are not fixed or absolute, but are marked (and re-marked) through relations and interactions among people, things, technologies, communities, meanings, spaces, and disciplines. In other words, boundary marks and relations both shape and are shaped by what gets made (and what doesn't), by whom, and for whom. Analyzing and understanding these marks, then, can help researchers, teachers, and practitioners make informed decisions about why and how to engage with the maker movement in our communities.

Consider, for example, that the boundaries that separate a human maker from a 3D printer are re-marked in a moment when the human uses her hand to help the machine feed plastic filament into its extruder as the machine prints. A writer who has previously not been regarded as a maker experiences a re-marking of boundaries as he learns and proves he can operate 3D printers and, in turn, is recognized as a maker. A researcher who had never seen a 3D printer before she started studying a makerspace notices that her early field notes relate what people are saying about 3D printers rather than what they are doing with 3D printers, but as she learns and becomes more familiar, the boundaries of her observations are re-marked to focus more on actions and processes, and not just words. And when a makerspace feels like a "total dudefest" (in the words of a man who lamented that fact to the only woman present in a makerspace that day), or is inaccessible to a person with a disability, then the boundaries of what is possible are opened up for some bodies, but closed down for other bodies. In other words, despite the name "makerspace," neither "maker" nor "space" is a given, but is continually and differently negotiated by different bodies. We must answer for these boundary marks in the theories, traditions, and practices of making we privilege in our communities, institutions, and classrooms.

Indeed, people who do not work in or interact directly with the maker movement are increasingly likely to encounter definitions of "making" and "maker" that are influenced by the maker movement in professional, community, and educational contexts. Public libraries and libraries in educational institutions are creating their own makerspaces, and the maker movement has attracted scholarly and pedagogical interest across disciplines and areas, including digital humanities, education, human-computer interaction, library and information science, business, and rhetoric and composition. In rhetoric and composition, my primary field, there is growing interest in making and makerspaces, as evidenced in increased representation in recent calls for proposals for conferences and collections and in the work of a growing body of researchers and teachers, including

Krystin Gollihue (2019), Maggie Melo (2018), Jentery Sayers (2017), David Sheridan (2010), John Sherrill (2014), Jason Tham (2019), and Stephanie West-Puckett (2017).

While this project engages primarily with perspectives on and studies of the relatively new maker movement, there are long histories and traditions of making that precede contemporary trends. As John Hagel, John Seely Brown, and Duleesha Kulasooriya (2013) explain,

> For millennia, people have been manipulating objects to suit their needs and transform the world around them. Our built world and the many inventions and innovations that populate it are testament to the long history of making. What is new is how modern technologies, globalization, and cultural shifts are enabling and motivating individuals to participate in making activities and removing barriers all along the value chain, from design and prototype to manufacturing to selling and distribution. (3)

Hagel, Brown, and Kulasooriya position the maker movement as the "next generation of inventing and do-it-yourself" (1), suggesting a lineage in twentieth-century hobby shop culture and the DIY movement of the late twentieth and early twenty-first centuries. Faythe Levine and Courtney Heimerl (2008) trace the maker movement through traditions of crafting and design beginning with the Arts and Crafts movement of the twentieth century. Jessamyn Hatcher and Thuy Linh Nguyen Tu (2017) more pointedly tie the contemporary maker movement to "the rise of neoliberalism, when problems of deindustrialization . . . were no longer addressed primarily through collectives—whether government, policy institutes, or unions—but instead devolved to individuals and businesses" (274). While the contemporary maker movement is situated in a specific technological, economic, and sociopolitical context, *making* resonates across time and contexts, as scholars of material culture like Tim Ingold have observed. Ingold (2013) defines making as "a process of correspondence: not the imposition of preconceived form on raw material substance, but the drawing out or bringing forth of potentials immanent in a world of becoming" (31). My study of a makerspace traces processes of becoming-through-making that include objects, bodies, technologies, relationships, and spaces.

In engaging with a local instantiation of the contemporary maker movement, this project builds on an emerging, cross-disciplinary body of work that examines the marking of difference in rhetorical practices of making. At the heart of this work is an understanding that neither the maker movement nor the technologies and objects associated with it are neutral. Rhetoric and composition scholars like Cynthia Selfe and Richard Selfe (1994), Adam Banks (2006), Angela Haas (2012), Laura Gonzales (2018a), and Jody Shipka (2011) have argued that technologies and our bodies' interactions with them are culturally situated. As Shipka (2011) argues, "We need to consider what is at stake—who and what it is that we empower or discount—when we use the term ["technology"] to mean primarily, or worse yet, *only* the newest computer technologies" (21). Furthermore, digital humanities scholar Jentery Sayers (2017), emphasizes the importance of redressing "the normative assumptions and effects of popular maker cultures—usually white, cisgender, straight, male, and able-bodied"—through critical interventions in and practices of making (7). And Debbie Chachra (2017), a materials scientist and engineering educator, makes a case against identifying as a "maker" because the "cultural primacy of making, particularly in tech culture—that it is intrinsically superior to not-making, repair, analysis, and especially caregiving—is informed by the gendered history of who is credited with making things, and, in particular, who made things that were shared with the world, not merely for hearth and home" (319).

In fact, by its own account—and despite efforts to the contrary from some within the movement—the maker movement skews heavily toward male-identified people. According to Maker Media's (2015) press fact sheet, 81% of the readers of *Make: Magazine* identified as male. And 70% of attendees at the 2014 Bay Area Maker Faire identified as male. Similarly, in Hackster.io's (2016) maker survey (in partnership with technology giants such as Intel, Microsoft, Google, Amazon, and Arm) of more than three thousand people across 104 countries, fewer than 7% of respondents identified as women. (Interestingly, neither Maker Media nor Hackster.io reported on race/ethnicity.) Additionally, scholars like JooYoung Seo and Gabriela Richard (2018) and Katherine Steele, Maya Cakmak, and Brianna Blaser (2018) point out the ways in which makerspaces and maker technologies can exclude people with disabilities, particularly when people with disabilities are not included in the process of planning and designing these spaces. While some identify makerspaces and maker practices as opportunities to bring underrepresented groups, such as women, into science, technology, engineering, and mathematics (STEM) fields (Blackley et al. 2017), others point to women's exodus from male-dominated makerspaces and hackerspaces to form women-centric spaces that promote feminist ways of making and collaborating (Fox, Ulgado, and Rosner 2015). The attention of these scholars to the underrepresentation of women in the mainstream maker movement resonates with the observations of scholars like Anne Balsamo (2011) and Sasha Costanza-Chock (2020) who trace broader accounts of erasures and exclusions of women and marginalized communities in technological innovation and design. For these reasons, I am wary, like education scholars Shirin Vossoughi, Paula Hooper, and Meg Escudé (2016), of the "uncritical adoption of branded versions of making, particularly with regard to their implications for education equity" (210).

Building on this scholarship, my observations and experiences from a makerspace, and the perspectives of the people with whom I worked, this book models a relational framework for understanding and participating in acts of making. This framework operates at multiple levels: the making and remaking of knowledge across theories, perspectives, and experiences; the making and remaking of bodies, relationships, meanings, technologies, and the makerspace itself; and the making and remaking of practices across local maker communities, the global maker movement, and maker-inspired pedagogies. At each level, I highlight relations and boundary marks that are dynamic, collaborative, multimodal, material, and culturally situated. In other words, while this book is a study of acts of making in a makerspace, it is also a study of how the boundaries of "maker," "making," and "knowledge" both shape and are shaped by relations among bodies, technologies, traditions, materials, things, and spaces. As a project that works across disciplines and across theory and practice, the book offers implications and applications of this relational framework for people who identify as makers, as well as community strategists and technical communicators, and also for writing teachers committed to supporting students' interests, backgrounds, and rhetorical skills.

Chapter Overview

The first portion of the book articulates a relational framework for making that includes making knowledge *about* making. Chapter 1 situates rhetoric and/as making, and it assembles understandings of relationality that guide my work. This chapter also introduces relational rhetorics as a way of participating in and accounting for relationships with and among bodies, spaces, theories, perspectives, and experiences. The theories, methodologies, practices, and relationships in this project are as much a part of the study phenomenon as the acts of making I examine. Drawing on traditions across epistemologies, Chapter 2 offers stories as a method/ology for relational rhetorics that offers not only my accounts and interpretations of experiences with makers and making, but also how I came to those accounts and interpretations and experiences. Readers who are interested in the dynamics and processes of qualitative research projects (like a longitudinal, ethnographically informed case study) will find in this chapter a detailed account of my philosophies, relationships, and techniques in conducting and writing about research on making.

The second portion of the book offers two chapters with stories from SoDo Makerspace. Readers interested in learning more about what I observed and experienced in my years studying a makerspace will find in these chapters stories about acts of making, rhetorical approaches to design and documentation, and dynamic relations among humans and machines in a makerspace over several years. These stories are my participation in (rather than my observation or representation of) the marking of boundaries. Enacting the method/ology described in Chapter 2, each story begins with a particular moment that came to matter to me and to the people I was interacting with. The stories trace how those particular moments came to matter, not only through the prior interactions that informed my understanding of and participation in that moment, but also through the ways in which that moment changed how I understood past and future interactions. I also connect these stories with the theoretical and methodological concepts discussed in Chapters 1 and 2.

Chapter 3 is a story of spatial manipulations (a phrase inspired by a 3D-printed "spatial manipulation toy"): interacting with people and objects, making objects, making space in a makerspace, and understanding embodied ways of meaning and making. The chapter focuses on the ways in which my own efforts to make space for myself in (or integrate myself into) a makerspace are entangled with how I understand what I observed there, particularly the efforts of Tony, a freelance writer, to make space for himself in the makerspace. And while Chapter 3 focuses on making things, Chapter 4 traces the complex function of disequilibrium (which includes breaking things) in making processes in SoDo Makerspace: from human errors and machine malfunctions to the amateur ethos of the space (and the maker movement) and systems of production. Some makers allow for and even cultivate a relatively high tolerance for disequilibrium as an invention practice. This story traces disequilibrium as both a marking of boundaries *and* a site for intervening in boundary marking. The threads of this story examine and account for disequilibrium-as-boundary-marking in machine operation and maintenance, in documentation practices, in prototyping and design, in the ethos of the space, and in production systems.

The third and final portion of this book looks beyond the physical space of SoDo Makerspace to trace relationships and practices of making. The relationships and ventures of makers are dynamic, and they exceed the physical and temporal space of a single makerspace, as Chapter 5 and the conclusion describe. In turn, my relationships and experiences in and beyond the makerspace shaped my approach to teaching writing and rhetoric, described in Chapter 6. Readers interested in the ways in which practices of making apply to professional and pedagogical work beyond makerspaces will find in these chapters discussions that illustrate these relationships and possibilities.

Chapter 5 focuses on professional practice in the maker movement and intersecting technology industries, and Chapter 6 focuses on iterations of a digital rhetorics course that was influenced by my research on making and relationships with makers. Both these chapters involve collaborative knowledge-making with my research participants and account not only for *what* we found in our collaborative analysis but also *how* we found what we found. In other words, just as Chapters 3 and 4 account for the making of my research(er) apparatus in SoDo Makerspace, these chapters account for the boundary-marking practices involved in collaborative knowledge-making in and beyond SoDo Makerspace, with implications for professional practice and for teaching. Thus, the methodology in this project can be useful not only for theorizing but also for (professionally) *doing* and *teaching* writing as complex, relational, material-discursive acts of making. Chapter 6 turns to implications for teaching by tracing the ways the concepts introduced in previous chapters shaped my approach to teaching writing and rhetoric. The stories in this chapter connect concepts like rhetoric as/and making, disequilibrium, spatial manipulations, stories, design, and community across my research and teaching practices to show the ways in which they informed each other. Finally, in the conclusion, I reflect on the affordances and constraints of this study and articulate future directions for the study, practice, and teaching of making.

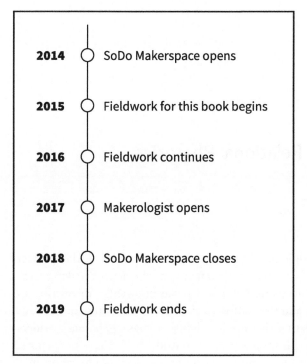

Figure 1. Chronology visualization: 2014–2019

Chronology Visualization: 2014–2019

While the stories in this book model a nonlinear, relational approach to knowledge making and storytelling, the visualization in Figure 1 presents a chronological narrative that emerges from and can be read alongside the nonlinear relations in the chapters, which move forward and backward in time to emphasize relationality. This chronological visualization provides a temporal orientation to the stories in this book.

CHAPTER ONE

Relational Rhetorics

The theories, methodologies, practices, and relationships in this project are as much a part of the study phenomenon as the acts of making I examine. This chapter accounts for how I make knowledge in relation to theoretical traditions and in relation to the communities this project engages. I begin by situating rhetoric in relation to making, because readers who come to this book from perspectives outside of the areas of rhetoric, composition studies, and technical and professional communication may be wondering what rhetoric has to do with a study of making. After all, in everyday language, "rhetoric" is usually synonymous with "razzle-dazzle style or verbal bullshittery," as Candice Rai (2016) aptly puts it (16). While there is plenty of razzle-dazzle and bullshit in the domain of rhetorics, I assemble an understanding of rhetorics in relation to making in order to provide a shared conceptual vocabulary for describing and participating in meaning-making work in and across makerspaces, classrooms, and professional and community contexts. I then assemble an understanding of relationality that works across epistemological traditions in conversation with experiences and perspectives from a makerspace. I conclude by presenting a framework of relational rhetorics that models a commitment to locating and pluralizing conceptual lenses for making—including making knowledge about making.

Rhetoric and/as Making

In situating rhetoric in relation to making, this book highlights two characteristics of rhetoric and making that are particularly salient to this study:

that they are both more than symbolic and more than human. By more than symbolic, I mean that both rhetoric and making involve doing, being, knowing, and relating using more than just words and other symbols. Whether we are in a makerspace or a writing classroom, we persuade, negotiate, solve problems, create, and act using a combination of words, symbols, objects, movements, spaces, and relationships. By more than human, I mean that both rhetoric and making involve doing, being, knowing, and relating beyond the intent and scope of human bodies. Again, whether we are in a makerspace or a writing classroom, the work of persuasion, negotiation, problem-solving, creation, and action includes forces, histories, and relationships that come from and circulate through more than just the bodies we recognize as human.

Much of what I have observed and engaged in during this study can be described as negotiating, persuading, solving problems, creating, and getting things done through acts of making with not only words and symbols, but also objects, movements, spaces, and relationships. These observations and experiences resonate with articulations of rhetoric like those offered by Angela Haas (2012), who defines rhetoric as "the negotiation of cultural information—and its historical, social, economic, and political influences—to affect social action (persuade)" (287), and Donnie Johnson Sackey (2018), who similarly describes rhetoric as "a means (tactics/tools) whereby people come together to solve localized problems in movement that frequently oscillates between local and global foci" (156). Jody Shipka (2011) draws attention to "other representational systems and ways of making meaning" than printed, spoken, and digital words (131), and David Sheridan (2010) argues specifically for attending to rhetoric in 3D objects (like those made in makerspaces), because objects, like words and symbols, can persuade and create meanings and actions (250). And while rhetorical scholars have long engaged with more-than-symbolic rhetorics across epistemological traditions, some have also taken up interdisciplinary work in new materialism to consider, as Ehren Pflugfelder (2015) does, "what rhetoric is like as we move beyond the humanist symbolic arts" (443). All these articulations expand a traditional focus in Western rhetorics on spoken and written words by suggesting that both the processes and the products of rhetoric can and do exceed symbolic forms. Therefore, while it might be surprising—as it was to participants in this study—that a researcher of writing and rhetoric would be interested in what happens in a makerspace, where the focus is on 3D objects, I am interested (like many researchers and teachers before me) in rhetoric and/as making with more than words, through the relations of objects, words, spaces, bodies, technologies, and meanings.

In this way, attending to more-than-symbolic rhetorics also draws our attention to the boundaries of what counts as rhetoric, because, as Sharon Crowley (1999) argues, "Distinctions and boundaries are never disinterested: when someone is named as a witch, a factory worker, a rustic, or an illiterate, someone else profits from that distinction. When images are distinguished from texts, someone profits. . . . no body is disinterested" (363). Excluding more-than-symbolic rhetorics in the boundaries we draw has consequences: for example, scholars like Ellen Cushman (2013) and Malea Powell (2012) have argued that restricting definitions of "rhetoric" or "literacy" to the realm of the alphabetic erases Indigenous peoples whose rhetorical and literate practices have (long before the rise of the contemporary maker movement) involved multimodal, embodied ways of meaning.

And just as excluding more-than-words in our definitions of rhetoric has consequences for whom we recognize and do not recognize as rhetorical, excluding traditions of making outside of the contemporary maker movement has consequences for whom we recognize and do not recognize as makers. Silvia Lindtner, Shaowen Bardzell, and Jeffrey Bardzell (2016) observe that technosolutionism, "the view that technology can unilaterally solve difficult social problems," is "visible in promotions of making that portray it as furthering sustainability, social justice for women, economic development for the Global South, and empowerment for all" (1390). Echoing Jessamyn Hatcher and Thuy Linh Nguyen Tu's (2017) point that the maker movement is tied to the rise of neoliberalism, Lindtner, Bardzell, and Bardzell observe that technosolutionism has consequences for practices of making that may not engage technologies in the ways privileged by technosolutionist definitions of making, because such practices might be then considered less empowering and less valuable. And as is the case in rhetoric, what counts as making is inextricably related to *who* counts.

This brings us to a second shared characteristic of rhetorics and practices of making: they are more than human in ways that can both enhance and erase bodies. Candice Rai (2016) describes rhetoric as "a force that not only orders our lives but also animates our bodies. Gets under our skin. Puts things into motion through and beyond human will. Emerging from and wedded to the co-constitutive interactions of language, people, things, matter, and all other presences and forces in the world" (16). Such an expansive view of rhetoric has, in turn, expanded how I experience and describe acts of rhetoric and making in a makerspace, because as Brian

McNely, Clay Spinuzzi, and Christa Teston (2015) observe, attending to more-than-human materialities troubles "how researchers . . . bound off and study objects and practices" (6).

Similarly, Jody Shipka (2016), drawing on the work of Laura Micciche, argues that more-than-human approaches to rhetoric help us redefine "multimodal collaborations 'as partnerships that include and exceed intentional ones established between people'—partnerships that involve the merging of 'various forms of matter' (Micciche 498)" (254). The merging of matter is particularly noticeable in a makerspace, and it echoes through a long history of making across cultures, as Tim Ingold (2013) observes: "In the act of making the artisan couples his [*sic*] own movements and gestures—indeed his very life—with the becoming of his materials, joining with and following the forces and flows that bring his work to fruition" (31). In the time I spent in makerspaces, I have seen objects and tools quite literally get under people's skin in ways that changed the outcomes of projects, and I have seen machines and materials exert as much influence on a process of making as the will and intent of humans.

And this all took place in an environment with lively and frequent conversations about human-machine integrations, often through science fiction analogies—as was the case in many of my conversations with a person I met at SoDo Makerspace who features prominently in this book: Tony Loiseleur, a writer and sociologist by training who is currently studying data science. Tony and I are both fans of the *Star Trek* franchise, and in one particular video-recorded conversation about the Borg (a cyborg collective and infamous antagonist in the franchise), Tony noted that the tools and technologies we make extend human capabilities and redefine what humans can be and do (Figure 2). "Sign me up!" Tony joked about the possibility of becoming a cyborg, but he added that he would want to be a cyborg "with feelings" (unlike the Borg).

I have learned from Tony to take a more than humanist but still human-centered approach to understanding and participating in making and rhetoric. By "more than humanist," I mean that I do not take the traditional Western humanist boundaries of who counts as "human" for granted, particularly since some bodies are recognized as more human or less human than others. And by "still human-centered," I mean that even as we dwell in the dynamic boundaries of "human" in relation with other bodies, machines, and environments, human bodies and relationships are both the point of reference and the focus of my work. After all, as Anne Frances Wysocki (2012) argues, "Our bodies—our primary media . . . are not fixed;

Figure 2. Tony works on a 3D printer and discusses human-technology relations

they are mutable. We come to be always already embedded—embodied—in mediation" (4). Therefore, a more than humanist but still human-centered approach foregrounds not only the making of technologies and objects, but also the making and remaking of bodies and relations—and all the possibilities and pitfalls entailed. Technologies are encoded with humans' values and biases, and technologies reinscribe and shape values and biases when we use them. And while technologies and acts of making can productively expand the boundaries of "human," I cannot ignore the dehumanizing effects of definitions of making that privilege certain bodies and traditions at the exclusion of others.

This boundary marking in definitions of rhetoric and making resonates with M. Remi Yergeau's (2017) observations about rhetoric in their work on autism:

> It is not uncommon . . . for rhetoricians to claim that rhetoric is what makes one human. This is a belief that persists in spite of rhetorical studies' various turns toward things, ecologies, affect, and complex vitalisms: if one is arhetorical, then one is not fully human. Rhetoric's function as a precondition for humanness or personhood is typically and deeply connected to how we conceive sociality, our modes of relating and relatedness with our (neurotypically human) surrounds. (6)

Extending Yergeau's observations about the persistent function of rhetoric as a precondition for humanness, I notice similar ways in which identifying and being identified as a "maker" has material and social consequences for which bodies belong—or matter—in the spaces and conversations of the maker movement. If, in the words of disability rhetorics scholar Margaret Price (2011), rhetoric is "who we are allowed to be" (27), making, likewise, is who are allowed to be. Yergeau's emphasis on neurotypicality also highlights the ways in which both definitions of rhetoric and definitions of making can normalize certain bodies as "able" to the exclusion of others, which in turn shapes the meanings and things that get made, for whom, and by whom. The "normal" human body envisioned in the design of spaces, machines, and interactions in a makerspace marks the boundaries of who can make, which in turn shapes what gets made.

Relationality

In drawing attention to the ways in which rhetoric and making are more than symbolic and more than human, I have emphasized that definitions of making and rhetoric mark boundaries that include who counts as rhetors and who counts as makers. These boundaries are both the mechanism and the product of unfolding relations. My vocabulary for conceptualizing these boundary marks through relations in a makerspace draws on conceptualizations of relationality across epistemological traditions, including the vocabulary of feminist scholar and physicist Karen Barad, whose work animates and is taken up in a number of conversations in and beyond rhetoric and writing studies. Like Leigh Patel (2015), I acknowledge that Barad's work "speaks first, and foremost, to Western technologies" and is thus "likely to connect most readily with Western-based readers" (51). Following the example of Patel, who includes Barad's work alongside Indigenous scholarship, and of Tara McPherson (2018), who reads Barad's work alongside the work of women-of-color and feminist scholars, I include Barad's work alongside Indigenous scholarship, intersectional feminist, disability studies, and queer scholarship not only in order to "connect to the entry points of many readers," as Patel puts it (52), but also to acknowledge that "citation practices and more fundamentally, epistemic genealogies hold material force in not just our histories but our possible futures" (52)—a point to which I will return in assembling my understandings of relationality.

Like other rhetoricians who have engaged Barad's work, I am compelled by the rhetorical possibilities in Barad's refusal to treat distinctions between human and nonhuman or subject and object as a given, as well as the rhetorical possibilities in her theory of agency as matter's entanglement across humans and nonhumans. But Barad (2007) is also careful to point out that simply including nonhumans alongside humans, or distributing agency symmetrically across humans and nonhumans, misses the ways in which, as Judith Butler puts it, "The construction of the human is a differential operation that produces the more and the less 'human,' the inhuman, the humanly unthinkable" (1993, 8; qtd. in Barad 2007, 59). Barad argues,

> Some science studies researchers are endorsing Bruno Latour's proposal for a new parliamentary governmental structure that invites nonhumans as well as humans, but what, if anything, does this proposal do to address the kinds of concerns that feminist, queer, postcolonial, (post-)Marxist, and critical race theorists have brought to the table? Nonhumans are in, but the concerns of this motley crew of theorists and activists seem not to have been heard, let alone taken into account. (58)

In other words—and as many feminist, Indigenous, queer, disability studies, and critical race theorists also argue—the differential markings of more or less human are as important as the markings of human and nonhuman.

Key to Barad's theorization of these differential markings through relations is the concept of "intra-action," in which the prefix "intra," as opposed to "inter," asserts "ontologically primitive relations—relations without preexisting relata" (139). In other words, there are not *a priori* subjects and objects that exist as stable, absolute entities outside of their engagements with and relations to each other. Instead, subjects and objects emerge— are continually marked and redefined—through their relations and intra-actions. Likewise, humans are continually marked and redefined as more or less human (more or less privileged) in intra-actions that are unfolding in each moment, context, and set of relations. These intra-actions, Barad argues, "materialize different phenomena—different marks on bodies," and therefore "do not merely effect what we know" but also "contribute to the differential mattering of the world" (178). Through these differential markings, some bodies are made to matter more than others; therefore, ethics and responsibility are inherent in intra-actions.

Barad's emphasis on a relational ethics of mattering through intra-action lends itself to critical, ethics-focused applications in theorizing and studying rhetoric, writing, and making. For example, Stephanie West-

Puckett (2017) found that Barad's concept of intra-action is useful in a study of making because it helps us to "reject an objective exteriority to knowing and being" (57). Julie Jung and Kellie Sharp-Hoskins (2017) build on Barad's work to articulate a "research ethic of emergent mattering" that insists that "*what* matters is premised on *how* it matters, that what matters has a history (i.e., it has been made to matter), and that what matters can matter differently" (x). Alison Cardinal (2019) draws on Barad's work to theorize participatory video methods through an understanding that "materiality, knowledge-production, and ethics are intertwined" (36). Indeed, as I observed machines mattering more, at times, than humans in a makerspace, Barad's emphasis on the ethics of mattering in intra-action is compelling as a way to describe the consequences of different relations and boundary marks among humans, as well as across humans and nonhumans. Barad's concept of intra-action is not merely about relating across difference, but treating the marking of difference itself as an intra-action—and therefore a space for negotiation.

And while these specific technological and theoretical configurations are relatively new, technologies as relations are not new, and neither are relational theories and ways of knowing. Jennifer Clary-Lemon (2019) argues that if we hold that "relationality is the primary way that meaning is made in the world," we must also be accountable for our relationships to knowledges beyond Eurocentric traditions (n.p.). Clary-Lemon's point echoes the work of Chela Sandoval (2000), who, nearly two decades earlier, argued that we must carefully account for the convergences in theoretical traditions from white, Western thinkers and from thinkers who "survived conquest, colonization, and slavery in order to develop insurgent theories and methods for outlasting domination" because "recognizing the alignments between these ideational forces becomes critical to the project of identifying citizen-subjects and collectives able to negotiate the globalizing operations of the twenty-first century" (6).

Therefore, just as the boundaries we draw around definitions of making and rhetoric have consequences, so too do the boundaries we draw around theoretical traditions. In other words, theorizing relationality from multiple epistemological traditions is an attempt to redress erasures in my knowledge-making practices, following Jennifer Sano-Franchini (2015), who calls us to account for what is privileged and what is silenced in the intellectual lineages we construct (23–24). Addressing epistemic genealogies (Patel 2015, 52) in theorizing relationality also aligns with the work Angela Haas (2012) lays out in the first part of her definition of decolonial methodologies, which "redress colonial influences on perceptions of people, literacy, language, culture, and community and the relationships therein" (297).

The second part of Haas's definition articulates another key methodological move in understanding relationality, which is to "support the co-existence of cultures, languages, literacies, memories, histories, places, and spaces—and encourage respectful and reciprocal dialogue between and across them" (297). José Cortez (2017) argues, similarly, that decolonial methodology "might be best understand as a practice of reading for the de-exceptionalism of all groups laying claim," cautioning that to position decoloniality as "an authentically non-Western voice" ultimately perpetuates an Aristotelian, binary model of tradition and resistance (59). Or, as Raúl Sánchez (2017b), puts it, "Description, in the form of [a] genuinely comparative approach . . . , is precisely what is needed if we want to theorize, study, and teach mark-making in a broader-than-merely alphabetic sense—that is, mark-making at the borders between Western Modernity and the Indigenous cultures of this hemisphere" (87).

I have used the word *decolonial* following the practice of rhetoric and composition scholars who approach this work "from the hope and vision that it is possible to explore 'border thinking,'" as Romeo García and Damián Baca (2019) put it (2), as a knowledge-making practice that decentralizes Western approaches. García and Baca draw upon the work of modernity/coloniality scholars like Walter Mignolo (2007), whose concept of "de-linking" is "a de-colonial epistemic shift leading to other-universality, that is, to pluri-versality as a universal project" (453). Still, Eve Tuck and K. Wayne Yang (2012) argue that "decolonization brings about the repatriation of Indigenous land and life; it is not a metaphor for other things we want to do to improve our societies and schools" (1). Responding to the exigence of Tuck and Yang's point, Leigh Patel (2014) posits that the term *anticolonial* "still allows for locating the hydra-like shape-shifting yet implacable logics of settler colonialism, but does not include in its semantic shape the unmet promises of stripping away colonization, as the term *decolonization* gestures to do. This, in itself, marks anticolonial stances as incomplete, as they don't necessarily address material change" (360). In this sense, *anticolonial* might more honestly describe the work and limitations of my project.

In engaging across traditions that theorize and intervene in more-than-symbolic, more-than-human rhetorics and relations, my goal is to locate the epistemologies that underpin those theorizations and interventions.

Attending to the ethics of mattering includes supporting the coexistence of theoretical frameworks and lived experiences (my own and those of people in my study) through respectful, reciprocal, de-exceptionalizing, comparative dialogue. To do this work, I am guided by scholars who acknowledge marginalized theoretical traditions and bring them together to highlight the explanatory power they offer. For example, in her account of creating accessible, multilingual digital content, Laura Gonzales (2018b) brings together the disability studies framework of interdependence and the framework of intersectionality, as articulated by legal scholar and Black feminist theorist Kimberlé Crenshaw. Drawing on the work of disability studies scholars Margaret Price and Stephanie Kerschbaum (2016), Gonzales explains that interdependent research methodologies "center 'care, commitment, and acting with others in mutually-dependent relationships,' where relying on others to access information is not a matter of choice but an intentional, necessary practice" (35). Gonzales goes on to explain that "the notion of interdependency as central to inclusive research practice also has a long, though differently-named, history in research on language and racial diversity," noting Crenshaw's work on intersectionality and the work of scholars of African American Language who show that "race, power, and language are always inherently tied and intertwined" (36). Indeed, Crenshaw (1989) has long argued that we need account not just for a single axis of difference (i.e., gender) but for the intersections and relations of different identities (i.e., gender, race, class, dis/ability, sexual orientation, etc.) and the harm experienced by people whose intersecting identities are marked as less human through structural, systemic discriminations.

In acknowledging and bringing together these frameworks, Gonzales shows how the concepts and traditions of intersectionality and interdependence complement and therefore can enrich her analysis and practice. The characteristics of intersectionality and interdependence that Gonzales highlights also enrich our understanding of relationality. Interdependence reminds us that dis/ability is constructed by the kinds of relationships we create (and specifically, the bodies we assume are "normal" and therefore design for), and that we need to recognize and be intentional about the ways our relations (among humans, technologies, bodies, environments) are interdependent. Intersectionality reminds us that identities are never separate from each other: my identity as a woman is never separate from my whiteness, my nondisabled status, my socioeconomic status as a university professor, or any of my other identities. Furthermore, while Barad's (2007) concept of intra-action emphasizes the dynamic and ever-unfolding nature of differential mattering, intersectionality reminds us to attend to patterns and histories of differential mattering, which we might recognize as structural and systemic discrimination. Or, as feminist media theorist Tara McPherson (2018) suggests, reading Barad's concepts alongside and in relation to theories of intersectionality moves Barad's concepts "more forcefully toward ways of theorizing difference" (100).

In addition (and in relation) to intersectional feminist and disability studies traditions, Indigenous traditions also guide my understanding of relationality. While Indigenous traditions are not monolithic, Shawn Wilson (2008) explains that "the shared aspect of an Indigenous ontology and epistemology is relationality (relationships do not merely shape reality, they are reality). The shared aspect of an Indigenous axiology and methodology is accountability to relationships" (7). Likewise, Gabriela Raquel Ríos (2015) reminds us that Indigenous approaches to relationality recognize that "humans and the environment are in a relationship that is co-constituted and not just interdependent" (64). Ríos's emphasis on co-constituting relations, which resonates with Barad's (2007) concept of intra-action, draws our attention to the ongoing, recursive marking of the boundaries of "human" and "environment" in and beyond a makerspace. Importantly, however, Ríos's land-based approach to relationality draws our attention not just to the context of humans and machines in a makerspace, but also specifically to the context of the colonial history of the land where this study took place.

Indeed, a book about boundary marking and relations would be remiss if it did not acknowledge not only the epistemological boundary markings of Western modernity and Indigenous cultures, but also the material, colonial boundary markings that shape the making of this book. Indigenous Peoples have long stewarded and continue to steward the lands on which I live and work as a white settler: in Seattle, Washington, on the traditional lands of the Duwamish and Coastal Salish Peoples, and in Tucson, Arizona, on the traditional lands of the Tohono O'odham and Pascua Yaqui Peoples. Angela Haas (2007) notes that "American Indian communities have employed wampum belts as hypertextual technologies . . . long before the 'discovery' of Western hypertext" (77), and the Indigenous cultures of this hemisphere likewise have technologies for and orientations to making that are often elided by the contemporary maker movement. For example, in an essay on making in the context of capitalism and settler colonialism, Dylan A. T. Miner (2019) explains,

At the core of my working with elders and youth is the phrase: *mawadisidiwag miinawaa wiidanokiindiwag //* they visit and work together. In this phrase there is nothing about making *aya'iin //* things. Rather it is about being together with one another and collectively learning from, with, and alongside each other. From an Indigenous way of being, the doing and being and making is far more important than what is actually made. (134)

And in an essay on composing and digital ethics, Kristin Arola (2018) draws upon experiences from a powwow and from years of working with American Indian women to articulate a practice of making that involves "putting yourself into the objects you bring into the world so as to honor the relations that came before and will come after" (275–276). While the makerspace I studied, like the institutions I work in, was situated in a neoliberal, settler-colonial context, the work of scholars like Ríos, Haas, Miner, and Arola teaches me to recognize and name that context as such, to examine my own "complicity in colonial practices" (Mukavetz 2018, 129), and to understand making (including research about making) through co-constituting relationships with people, spaces, lands, and meanings.

Furthermore, the recursivity inherent in a relational orientation resonates with Violet Livingston's (2015) articulation of queer rhetorics of consent, which has enriched how I understand and navigate relationality in engaging with study participants. As Livingston explains,

Consent is queer-based community rhetoric, and has the potential to provide queer frameworks for writing teachers and rhetoric scholars to think about ethical relationships. Queer rhetorics invite us to know consent as a collaborative, self-reflexive process, not simply a fleeting conversation about the benefits and risks of relationships that happens at the beginning of play. What I want to suggest is: consent [is] also a set of practical elements, which are part of ongoing, rhetorical negotiations where people can come to know their own power, privilege, and desires, and use them well. (16)

This articulation also resonates with the negotiation emphasized in Haas's (2012) definition of rhetoric, as well as Barad's (2007) conceptualization of intra-actions as unfolding relations. Livingston's emphasis on ongoing, rhetorical negotiations in relationships draws our attention to our relationships not only with theoretical traditions but also with the lived experience and perspectives of the people we interact with in our research.

Indeed, my understanding of relationality is also informed by the knowledges and practices of the people I met and collaborated with in this study, including Clarissa San Diego, founder and CEO of Makerologist. My relationship with Clarissa transformed how I understand and practice making, because she takes a relational approach to engaging people, technologies, machines, and things. For example, in Chapter 4, she describes her interaction with a CNC (computer-numerical control) routing machine as an intimate relationship that involves negotiations. And in Chapter 5, she shows how she applies relational prototyping strategies—including negotiation—both to creating human connections and to creating 3D objects. In learning not only from theoretical traditions but also from the knowledge and practice of Clarissa, a woman of color whose perspectives are underrepresented in the maker movement, I follow a tradition of feminist rhetorical scholarship, as articulated by Jacqueline Jones Royster and Gesa Kirsch (2012), of listening to and being guided by the work and words of women from whom we have much to learn (649).

Adam Banks (2011) has made a similar argument about work in digital rhetorics and computers and composition: "Any attempt to foster meaningful access to communication technologies or to a working education system must include theoretical frameworks or conceptual models that build from the traditions and truths of a people and assume their agency and ability" (5). This is particularly important in amplifying definitions and practices of making that include more bodies than those most often represented in makerspaces and the maker movement. Likewise, technical and professional communication scholars like Victor Del Hierro (2018) seek to build theories, as well as tools and technologies, that are "community-driven, localized, and accessible to a wide range of audiences" (11). If my goals are (a) to speak not only to academics but also to people in and beyond the maker movement, and (b) to participate in the work of expanding the voices and perspectives by which "making" and the "maker movement" are defined, then I must learn from and amplify the knowledge-making work of practitioners like Clarissa and her colleagues.

Relational Rhetorics

My approach to relationality, rhetorics, and making seeks to account for boundary marking both in the construction of concepts, lineages, and methodologies, and in phenomena like acts of making in a makerspace. This means continually asking not only "What counts as making?" and "Who counts as a maker?" but also "What counts as knowledge?" and "Who counts as a knowledge maker?" And when I refer to boundary marking, I do not mean to suggest that boundaries are fixed, absolute, or given, but rather that they are felt, relative, and negotiated. Instead, I follow the example of Barad (2007), who emphasizes that boundaries are continually unfolding, and of Fatima El-Tayeb (2011), who offers "fuzzy edges and intersections" as a more fruitful alternative to fixed boundaries that allows for "the exploration of commonalities while paying close attention to specific circumstances" (47–48). Therefore, this project engages in the fuzzy edges and unfolding boundary marks of definitions, epistemologies, and relationships in the making of a study about making. I describe this work, which is both a process and product, as relational rhetorics because this work

- brings together multiple theories, perspectives, and experiences from multiple bodies and spaces;
- places theories, perspectives, and experiences into dialogue; and
- participates in and accounts for relationships with and among bodies, spaces, theories, perspectives, and experiences.

Rhetoric is relational. *What* and *how* we know and do is inseparable from *where, when, in what bodies,* and *with whom* we know and do. As Angela Haas (2012) notes, "Every culture has its own rhetorical roots, traditions, and practices," and thus rhetoric "takes into account that subjectivity and knowledge are interrelated" (287). Haas draws on the work of Lucy Suchman (2002), who argues that design is a "vision from somewhere" that is "inextricably based in an embodied, and therefore partial, perspective—which makes us personally responsible for it" (96). Design includes not only the objects designed and made in a makerspace, but also the theories and methods used to design knowledge about making. In other words, if a theory or design is presented as a vision from everywhere (or nowhere)—one that is universally explanatory—then the specific conditions and bodies that produced that theory or design are made to stand in for all conditions and bodies in ways that can be limiting at best and harmful at worst. Instead, Suchman argues (as have many before her) that we need to acknowledge and take responsibility for the fact that theories are necessarily partial because they come from someone, somewhere.

Not only are theories partial in the sense that they are not whole, but they are also partial in the sense that they actively shape the knowledge we make using those theories. Juan Guerra (2013) reminds us that "we find what we look for, and we look for what the conceptual lenses we use allow us to see" (83). To acknowledge and mitigate the inevitable partiality of my own theoretical engagement, I locate and pluralize the conceptual lenses I use. This approach is informed by the "interfaces" model set forth by Casie Cobos, Gabriela Raquel Ríos, Donnie Johnson Sackey, Jennifer Sano-Franchini, and Angela Haas (2018) in their discussion of cultural rhetorics, which works to "move away from prescriptivist and singular definitions" (141). In locating and pluralizing conceptual lenses, I do not mean to suggest that all the parts I assemble add up to a universal whole, or that biases have been eliminated. Rather, by locating and pluralizing conceptual lenses, I am highlighting the fact that they are parts.

An emphasis on locatedness and plurality is fitting to a study of making, because the maker movement is not a monolith. Silvia Lindtner, Shaowen Bardzell, and Jeffrey Bardzell (2016) argue that the term *maker movement* is "often presented as a global universal, applying equally to Silicon Valley, Taipei, Changsha, and Windhoek" when, in fact, making is better understood as a "global assemblage" of practices that bear a "family resemblance" but are grounded in different cultural, geographic, and economic contexts (1392). Just as practices of making are multiple, theoretical traditions are multiple. I seek to engage across traditions following the practice of constellation, as articulated by the Cultural Rhetorics Theory Lab (2014): "building relationships between multiple traditions, multiple histories, multiple practices" (7).

To enact this relationship building, I am guided by Adela Licona and Karma Chávez's (2015) figuring of relational literacies as "the labor of making meaning, of shared knowledges, or of producing and developing new knowledges together" (n.p.). Just as Haas emphasizes the locatedness and relatedness of rhetorics, Licona and Chávez define relational literacies as "understandings and knowings in the world that are never produced singularly or in isolation but rather depend on interaction" (n.p.). Therefore, I use the phrase *relational rhetorics* to locate both the process and product of my engagement across theories and practices, my own experiences and observations of making, and the perspectives and experiences of participants in the study.

If my goal is to account for the locatedness and plurality of knowledge-making practices, then instead of treating theories and methods as something to apply to the study of a phenomenon, I must treat theories and methods as themselves part of the phenomenon, both shaping and shaped by what happens in the study. In this way I follow Raúl Sánchez's (2017a) articulation, drawing on the work of Bruno Latour, of a reimagined empiricism for knowledge making that moves beyond applying a theoretical framework to an object of study:

> Instead, we would constantly articulate and rearticulate *relations* between and among the various components (including ourselves and our frameworks) in constantly proliferating and changing systems. According to Latour, these components "make everything, including their own frames, their own theories, their own contexts, their own metaphysics, even their own ontologies," and it would be the task of a new empiricism to never stop writing them up as thoroughly as possible, recognizing every framework or interpretation as itself a part of the system being described rather than a privileged perspective onto that system. (6–7)

Echoing Licona and Chávez's emphasis on the inseparable relations of knowings and interactions, Sánchez highlights the recursive, co-constituting nature of these relations in the act of writing about knowledge making. My commitment to engaging thoroughly with these recursive relations is at the heart of my efforts to tell stories that not only relate experiences and findings from a makerspace, but also relate the conditions of the stories' own making. I do this as a way of locating not only the conceptual lenses I draw upon, but also my own positionality as a knowledge maker, because, as Steven Alvarez (2019) argues, it is important to work against "the colonizing gaze of the decontextualized researcher and the accompanying rhetoric that normalizes a 'universal' viewpoint" (86).

Readers may have noticed, by this point, that I have framed much of the content of this book as stories. This is because stories are key to the process and product of relational rhetorics in this book. Indeed, Rebecca Walton, Kristen Moore, and Natasha Jones (2019) argue that "stories are sites of knowledge making, theory building, and relational work" (xxi). Stories also figure in the "four points of practice" that Phil Bratta and Malea Powell (2016) argue should be "worked together" in cultural rhetorics scholarship: these four points of practice are "decolonization, relations, constellation, and story" (n.p.). Stories are how I share accounts and interpretations of experiences in and beyond a makerspace, as well as how I came to those accounts and interpretations, because my participation as a researcher and storyteller is what Barad (2007) describes as an intra-action that brings about differential matterings (178). My approach to story making also resonates with what digital humanities scholar Matt Ratto (2011) calls "critical making," a practice that "theoretically and pragmatically connect[s] two modes of engagement with the world that are often held separate—critical thinking, typically understood as conceptually and linguistically based, and physical 'making,' goal-based material work" (253). Ratto describes critical making in the context of collaborative work of digital humanities scholars to interrogate, test, and build critical theories through the work of making physical prototypes. In my case, the many acts of making I observed and the many acts of making I myself engaged in—learning how to fabricate 3D objects, creating the digital content for this book, building relationships and understandings with people, and writing (and rewriting) these words—both shape and are shaped by theories, concepts, and conversations. Stories, then, are how I do and show the work of critical making. In the next chapter, I situate stories—drawing across epistemologies and practices—as a method/ology for relational rhetorics that can help us account and answer for boundary-marking practices in acts of making in scholarly conversations, in makerspaces, in communities, and in classrooms.

CHAPTER TWO

Stories

On a chilly afternoon in March 2016, I watched as Tony Loiseleur—lead writer for SoDo Makerspace's blog at the time—directed the composition of a video. The video was shot by another makerspace regular, who was perched on a tall ladder and using the then-new Instagram app Boomerang, which records a burst of photos and plays them forward and backward on repeat. The video featured a new fan installed high on the front wall of the space above the garage door, which usually stayed closed during Seattle's long cool season. The fan vented fumes from the makerspace's machines and materials, as well as unwanted paint fumes from the shop next door.

"I'm trying to write a blog post that doesn't sound like our neighbors are trying to kill us," Tony explained, jokingly. "I'm trying to make it sound like a nice place to come visit."

"Rhetoric in the making," I joked back.

"There is a lot of fabrication involved," Tony replied. As I laughed at the apt pun and wrote down our exchange in my notebook, Tony nodded at my notebook and added, "And there's your soundbite."

This chapter begins with Tony's soundbite to illustrate the multiple dimensions of stories in this book. These stories relate experiences in and beyond a makerspace to readers. But the stories also relate experiences to each other and to theoretical frameworks (and epistemologies), and they relate the making of stories themselves. This particular story, Tony's soundbite, invites readers to imagine themselves with Tony and me in the makerspace, trying to make light of toxic fumes. The story also relates to definitions of rhetoric: Tony's fabrication pun not only echoes David Sheridan's (2010) concept of "the rhetoric of fabricated objects" (250), but also plays on the everyday definition of rhetoric as "razzle-dazzle style and verbal bullshittery," as Candice Rai (2016) puts it (16). And finally, the story highlights the dynamics of its own making: Tony and I were in conversation not only about what was going on in the makerspace, but also about the stories we were both trying to tell about what was going on in the makerspace.

Stories are an integral part of the process and product of relational rhetorics in my study. As I have explained, relational rhetorics

- bring together multiple theories, perspectives, and experiences from multiple bodies and spaces;
- place these theories, perspectives, and experiences into respectful dialogue; and
- participate in and account for relationships with and among bodies, spaces, theories, perspectives, and experiences.

This chapter offers stories as a method/ology for relational rhetorics in a study of making. Because the word "methodology" can mean different things (not unlike the word "rhetoric"), I want to clarify what I mean. Martin Hammersley (2011) explains that methodology can refer to techniques, philosophies, or a researcher's autobiography of approaches. Rather than treating these as separate categories, I understand methodology to encompasses all three categories, which is why I write it as "method/ology." Following traditions across epistemologies that emphasize the inseparability of knowing and doing, I view method/ology as the nonlinear, co-constituting relations of philosophies and techniques, as well as the stories I tell about those philosophies and techniques. Therefore, the sections of this chapter connect my philosophies of relational rhetorics with autobiographies of my approaches and techniques. These sections and stories highlight three important characteristics of stories: that they are active and dynamic, that they are multiple and relational, and that they are more than human and more than linear.

Active and Dynamic

To contextualize my use of the word "story," I share definitions across epistemological traditions that both shape and are shaped by practices and experiences in the context of my work, just as I have done with definitions of relational rhetorics. Malea Powell (2012), building on the work of Lee

Maracle, explains that a story is "an event in which I try to hold some of the complex shimmering strands of a constellative, epistemological space long enough to share them with you" (384). Drawing on Indigenous traditions, Powell emphasizes the active, co-constituting work of stories in a way that echoes Shawn Wilson's (2008) point that in Indigenous ontologies and epistemologies, "relationships do not merely shape reality, they are reality" (7). Similarly, from a Western feminist-materialist perspective, Karen Barad (2007) argues for an "onto-epistem-ology—the study of practices of knowing in being" (185).

Powell's definition resonates with my experiences on many levels. As I struggled initially to understand and relate in a makerspace, stories created space for me: people shared their stories with me, and I began to find ways to identify with people and practices. Likewise, the stories I could tell about making became important for creating shared space with readers and audiences who are unfamiliar with the maker movement. And the mechanism for creating this shared space was a knowing-in-being approach to accounting for knowledges, experiences, perspectives, and relationships.

I also came to understand that the creation of shared space was happening not only in the telling of stories, but also in the making of stories—and that accounting for the making of stories is part of telling stories. To this end, Barad (2007) calls for "genealogical analyses not only of the multiple apparatuses of bodily production that come to matter but also of the changing nature of the dynamics itself" (242). Those changing dynamics necessarily include the storyteller's relationship to and participation in the unfolding story. Barad's approach to genealogy thus reworks objectivity by committing to ways of knowing that "do not seek to uncover the truth of the past but rather are interested in the conditions of the possibility of truth making" (474 n. 68). Sharon Stevens (2004) applies Barad's theoretical work to the practice of using ethnographic techniques like observations and interviews to study rhetoric in a particular context. Like Powell, Stevens emphasizes that the stories and knowledge that come from such an approach are not passive reflections of a preexisting reality, but rather are active cocreations of knowledges and realities. Brenton Faber (2002) similarly describes his participatory approach to technical and professional communication research: "Change itself is a story, and stories are acts of change" (21). These approaches remind us that the gathering and telling of stories is an active and dynamic process, as it creates new understandings, new realities, and new possibilities. To illustrate these characteristics, I describe changing dynamics in the design of this study in the following paragraphs. I also attend to the active and dynamic nature of storytelling throughout this book by interweaving the "how" and "what" of stories (how I arrived at the story, as well as what happened and what we can learn from the story).

I first began conceptualizing a study with SoDo Makerspace in Seattle as my primary field site in 2015, while I was working on my PhD at the University of Washington. When I first asked Eric Renn, founder and CEO, for permission to study the space in March 2015, I told him that I was developing a project on the relationships among writing, rhetoric, and making. I also told him that I planned to use ethnographic methods, including interviews, textual and physical artifact collection, and observation (with a heavy emphasis on the latter, particularly at first). And I told him that I wanted to be useful by helping, if help was needed, with communication and by documenting and sharing the unfolding stories of SoDo Makerspace. Just as Tony advocated for the importance of storytelling (through the SoDo Makerspace blog) as a way to help people connect to the space, Eric, too, embraced the idea of documenting and sharing stories of the space. Therefore, my study and the stories in this book begin at SoDo Makerspace, which opened its doors in September 2014 and closed in October 2018 (Figure 1).

Because my relationships with the people in this study started at SoDo Makerspace and extended beyond its walls and, eventually, beyond its life span, I want to offer an orientation to the spaces in which I came to understand making. Founded by Eric Renn, who describes himself as a serial social entrepreneur, in 2014, SoDo Makerspace was located in Seattle's industrial SoDo neighborhood, near the Stadium District. The physical hub was in a warehouse space on Occidental Avenue. The main space, known as the Community Classroom, was a 2,000-square-foot open warehouse space full of machines, tools, art, materials, and projects. The appearance of the space changed frequently over four years, as did many of the people and projects in the space. The space was anchored by its fabrication technologies: a suite of 3D printers, a laser cutter, a soft-goods lab with industrial sewing machines, a small electronics lab, a large CNC (computer-numerical control) router and mini-CNC routers, a collection of tools, and a collection of refurbished computers. On the wall opposite the 3D printers and laser cutter, there were whiteboards that were sometimes completely covered in writing and drawings, and sometimes almost completely blank. Near these whiteboards was a large table where people met, worked, played games, taught, and learned. Toward the back were storage areas and workspaces of the people who were part of the regular operations. These people frequently taught certification classes on the various machines in the space and offered workshops on techniques ranging from small electronics to laser cutting and CNC milling (both sources of revenue). During my fieldwork at SoDo Makerspace, I witnessed tours (like the one I was on when I first visited), certifications, meetings, workshops, production on client-commissioned projects, tinkering with machines and prototypes, repairs on machines and building features, and even a music concert.

From March 2015 until June 2016, I visited SoDo Makerspace as regularly as possible to document the changing dynamics of the space itself because, as Candice Rai (2016) explains, "Fieldwork helps us examine the ways that rhetoric manifests from and circulates consequentially within the dynamic places, practices, ideologies, relationships, and material conditions of everyday life" (15). Through my initial fieldwork, I achieved my goal of what Sarah Read (2011) calls a "low but steady level" of physical presence, which allowed me to inhabit both "micro and macro levels" of stories and dynamics, "without losing site of either one" (46). This was especially important as I worked to familiarize myself with an unfamiliar space and unfamiliar technologies and to build relationships with people.

In fact, I spent much of 2015 learning how to understand and interact with the people and machines I encountered in SoDo Makerspace. Despite being warmly welcomed into the space as a researcher by Eric, I struggled initially to feel that I fit into the space. I had no prior connection to anyone in the space, I had no idea how any of the machines worked, and I was often the only woman-identified person in the space. Slowly but surely, I learned how the machines worked and connected with people in the space. Through these relationships, I felt more and more at ease in the space. With these foundational relationships established, after June 2016, my fieldwork transitioned to checking in periodically with focal participants by electronic communication and site visits. The site visits became less frequent when I moved away from Seattle in summer 2017 to work at the University of Arizona.

As the dynamics of my fieldwork and of SoDo Makerspace itself changed, so, too, did the scope of the study. I became increasingly curious about cofounders and volunteers whom I'd met and learned about in my early visits but who were no longer in the space. Therefore, in January 2016, I reached out to two women I'd met briefly in early 2015, and the scope of my study expanded beyond the walls of SoDo Makerspace. That same month, I also first visited the MyOpen3D workshop in January 2016 on a field trip from SoDo Makerspace with Eric Renn and Alex Cheker, who runs the MyOpen3D workshop and was at the time also working out of SoDo Makerspace. Alex, who designs and sells open-source 3D printers and kits, had offered to show us his workshop, and Eric was eager for shop design inspiration. The workshop was half of a shared basement space owned by Alex's friend, an artist. When we walked in, Eric was immediately delighted by Alex's organization of his space, especially his skillful use of shelving and labeled boxes. In addition to a computer station and workbench, the MyOpen3D shop had a table in the middle of the space, a whiteboard on the wall opposite the computer station, a suite of 3D printers on a large shelving unit, and a laser cutter.

It would be more than a year before I returned to the MyOpen3D workshop, this time in May 2017. Alex and Tony Loiseleur (who had also previously been at SoDo Makerspace) were working primarily from the MyOpen3D space and were focusing on Alex's 3D printer and kit business. That same year, SoDo Makerspace cofounder Clarissa San Diego founded Makerologist, a collective of entrepreneurs, most of whom had met at SoDo Makerspace. In November 2017, Alex made the workshop available for weekly open hours to the Makerologist team. And that, according to Clarissa, is "when the magic began" for the Makerologist team. As the Makerologist team grew, Clarissa and some of her Makerologist colleagues went in together on an office space in Impact Hub Seattle (in Seattle's Pioneer Square neighborhood), which is part of an international network of coworking spaces that emphasize positive social contributions.

I first visited Impact Hub Seattle in January 2018, when Clarissa and her colleagues were touring possible offices in the space. They decided on an office space and began gathering furniture, tools, and materials for their space. Many of the team members maintained their own workspaces (like the MyOpen3D workshop) in addition to the Impact Hub Seattle, which functions as a coworking and meeting space for the team. In April, July, and September 2018, I attended team meetings and coworking time in several spaces in Impact Hub Seattle, including the Makerologist office, a nearby conference, and common areas. In September 2018, I also visited SoDo Makerspace one last time before it closed the following month. And while I have followed makers and their work beyond the walls of their workshop spaces, SoDo Makerspace, the MyOpen3D workshop, and the Makerologist office in Impact Hub Seattle were key physical spaces in this study.

But digital spaces were also important for the ongoing work of this study and my relationships with participants. Particularly in months when I was less physically present, I kept up with people and activities through digital spaces: social media, productivity apps, and email. For example, I kept up with Eric and SoDo Makerspace regulars through email, social media, the SoDo Makerspace blog, the SoDo Makerspace Trello board, the SoDo Makerspace Slack workspace. Similarly, I kept up with Clarissa, Tony, and the Makerologist team via email, social media, video conferencing, and the Makerologist Slack.

In sharing these stories of visits, spaces, organizations, and scopes in the study, my point is to emphasize that I did not simply bound off a study site and time period and document what happened. After all, the phenomenon of making in and beyond a makerspace is exemplary of what Clay Spinuzzi (2015) and other scholars have described as an adhocracy, in which professionals rely increasingly on their highly connected (but also highly permeable) networks instead of the structures of a traditional, hierarchical bureaucracy. Relatedly, as I have noted, Jessamyn Hatcher and Thuy Linh Nguyen Tu (2017) tie the maker movement to "the rise of neoliberalism, when problems of deindustrialization . . . were no longer addressed primarily through collectives—whether government, policy institutes, or unions—but instead devolved to individuals and businesses" (274). In other words, dynamic spaces and relations (like those in neoliberal adhocracies in and beyond the maker movement) both call for and shape dynamic method/ologies. Dynamic method/ologies, in turn, shape understandings and representations of the spaces and relations. These changing dynamics also created new ways of gathering and telling stories.

Multiple and Relational

The changing dynamics in adhocracies like SoDo Makerspace and Makerologist mean that there are different voices and configurations of people (and technologies and spaces) over time. Thus, while I began my study by focusing on SoDo Makerspace, my decision to seek out and keep up with people who left SoDo Makerspace led to a multiplicity not only of sites but also of perspectives. Stories became a powerful tool not only for understanding identifications but also disidentifications (disavowals) and nonidentifications (neither avowing nor disavowing), to draw on Krista Ratcliffe's (2005) terms. In this sense, I embraced the fact that, as Natasha Jones and Rebecca Walton (2018) argue, "stories are relational, taking into account a number of actors, perspectives, time periods, and ethical views. The relational aspect of narratives make them well suited to not only conveying complex contexts but to understanding those contexts" (255).

Therefore, rather than attempting to create a single story myself or allowing one participant's story to speak for all, I sought to "[grow] different stories alongside one another," as John Law (2002) models in his story-based approach to sociological examination (5). The result, Law explains, is that

> we create and make visible interferences between the stories. We bring new and unpredictable effects into being, effects which cannot be predicted or foretold from a single location. New forms of subjectivity. To do this is to alter the character of knowing and writing. It is to render them multiple, decentered, or partially centered, in this place that refuses both modernism and postmodernism. (5)

Law's emphasis on multiplicity and partiality echoes the work of decolonial and feminist scholars who place perspectives and experiences in reciprocal, de-exceptionalizing dialogue (Haas 2012) and who emphasize that perspectives come from somebody (Suchman 2002).

Linda Tuhiwai Smith (1999) argues, drawing on the work of Russell Bishop, that Indigenous practices of storytelling offer researchers a model for "representing the 'diversities of truth' within which the story teller rather than the researcher retains control" (145). Natasha Jones (2016) applies a similar approach in narrative inquiry, which she argues "can be used as a tool that engages feminist perspectives in a critical manner, providing researchers with rich data that has the ability to call into question existing knowledge, voices and silence, and perceptions" (479–480). These approaches emphasize that a multiplicity of perspectives told through stories can productively denormalize and highlight the situatedness of perspectives, including and especially the researcher's. In this book, the voices and stories of the people I met and collaborated with offer different perspectives that come from different relationships to making, as well as to me and to each other.

All these understandings of story making helped me account for the ways in which my own positionality (including my dynamic relationships with spaces, technologies, and people) and the positionalities of the people I worked with shaped the process of growing stories alongside each other, to return to Law's words. For example, while being the only woman in

SoDo Makerspace for much of my fieldwork there shaped how I felt and related in the space, this is not the whole story. Through the lens of intersectionality (Crenshaw 1989) I understand that my identity as a woman is never separate from my more privileged identities, including my whiteness, my nondisabled status, and my status as a university-employed researcher. Therefore, as I seek to participate ethically in spaces and relations, I have been guided by Natasha Jones, Kristen Moore, and Rebecca Walton's (2016) framework for "interrogating how social and ideological identity markers (like race, gender, sexuality, and ableness) are coconstructed and shaped by what we call the 3Ps" (212). Those 3Ps are *positionality*, *privilege*, and *power*. As a researcher, attending to the 3Ps means not only describing what I encounter but also accounting for my own 3Ps and amplifying marginalized voices, both in the theories and methodologies I draw upon and in the stories I tell.

Therefore, I describe the dynamics of story making in this study, tracing approaches I took to document stories and co-tell stories. Indeed, much of my focus in the first year of the study was figuring how best to document stories in the makerspace. I felt very much like an outsider, as I was new both to the maker movement and to this particular makerspace, but I also had a familiar way of inhabiting that outsider feeling. Before I became an academic, I was a writer for a regional lifestyle magazine, parlaying the journalism skills I learned as a reporter for my undergraduate university newspaper into the work of telling stories about people, places, and events for the magazine. Thanks to my experience in journalism, I was familiar with being unfamiliar, so I turned to observation and documentation—not only in the journalistic traditions I had practiced professionally, but also in the research traditions I engage as an academic—as my primary modes of being and relating, especially in the first year of the study. And over time, my orientations to observation and documentation shifted as I built relationships with the participants in the makerspace, so that what I observed (and what I document in this book) came to include my relationships to the people and spaces around me.

My goal in this four-year study was to attend not only to the making of technologies and objects, but also to the making and remaking of bodies, rhetorics, and relations. In other words, the acts of making through which objects and technologies are designed and produced are also acts of marking the boundaries of bodies, things, and rhetorics. These acts involved a complex array of relations among bodies, knowledges, economies, gestures (human and machine), languages (including programming languages), tools, materials, and physical spaces. As I observed and documented these acts of making, I found myself relying on an array of tools and approaches to account for the dimensions of making. By dimensions of making, I mean not only the three dimensions of Euclidian space, but also a fourth dimension of time, as well as the dimensions of the complex array of relations I described above.

In December 2015, after nearly a year of spending time in SoDo Makerspace, I decided to augment my handwritten notes and photographic records with video footage captured on a body-worn camera (i.e., a Go-Pro worn on a strap on my head). My rationale was that the affordances of video could help me record and relate experiences in a makerspace to people who might be unfamiliar with such a space, and these affordances could help me attend to dimensions of making in my own analysis and telling of stories. By wearing the camera on my head (in a manner inspired by the growing use of body-worn cameras to capture first-person perspective in sports and adventures), I aimed to draw attention to my own embodied, emplaced view as a researcher. Furthermore, the regulars in the space were, by then, used to my taking notes and taking pictures and videos (with permission) via handheld devices, so I figured that showing up with a video camera on my head would be strange, but not totally unsettling. One day that December, I video-observed (again, with permission) Richard Albritton, one of the cofounders of SoDo Makerspace, using the laser cutter to make a dress form for displaying his cosplay creations (Figure 3). The laser beam was moving toward a part of the plywood sheet that was warped, and because the machine is calibrated in a way that assumes the material is lying flat on the cutting bed, Richard used his fingers to press the warped edge of the plywood flat as the laser beam passed by.

There are multiple layers of relations and boundary markings at play here, and many of them exceed the verbal interaction Richard and I had as he worked. On the one hand, there are dimensions to this interaction that would be difficult to capture in words alone and are highlighted in the video, such as the sound of the laser cutter, the tone of our voices, the nuances of Richard's posture and movements, and my own placement and gaze in the interaction. On the other hand, there are dimensions to this interaction that could not be captured in the video. While Richard reminded me to "do as I say, not as I do," I realized that Richard's experiences operating the SoDo Makerspace laser cutter for more than a year had given him a keen sense of how the machine worked, of the problems that would occur when the laser passed over warped material, and of spatial relations like the

Figure 3. Richard operates the laser cutter

airflow space at the front of the machine (just wide enough for fingers) and where the laser beam would move along the toolpath he had specified in the driver.

Since Richard's expertise was also acknowledged by his colleagues, no one else in the makerspace reacted to Richard's risky move. By contrast, in machine demonstrations for visitors and machine certification trainings, people are shown how to flatten warped material using clamps. No one told Richard to stop or be careful, even though his decision to put his fingers inside the machine near the path of the laser beam was not protocol. In other words, what is *not* said in the video matters, just as the fact that he easily accomplished his goal of flattening the board without being injured matters. In the acts of recording and rewatching these multiple dimensions of making, I was reminded that the mark of a maker is not only the embodied, proprioceptive knowledge of machine movements, but also the shared recognition of one's expertise (which is also related to the recognition of one's privilege).

But there is another important boundary-marking relation in this story: my own involvement in the interaction. When I first began researching the makerspace, I was unfamiliar with the fabrication technologies in the space:

I had never seen, much less operated, a laser cutter, 3D printer, or CNC milling machine. I spent the first several months of my fieldwork learning to understand and communicate not only with the people in the space, but also with the machines. This moment with Richard happened nearly nine months into my fieldwork, by which point I had an understanding both of Richard and of the laser cutter. What the camera does not show is that as Richard put his hands in the machine, my eyes widened, because I knew the risk involved. But because I also knew his ethos as a maker, I expressed my surprise as a joke ("Living on the edge!" as opposed to "What are you doing?!"). In other words, my own prior embodied experiences with the laser cutter and interacting with people in the space made it possible for me to know what Richard was doing and that what he was doing was risky.

To account for these relational boundary markings in this video-recorded interaction, I considered our verbal interactions, our gestures and movements, the marking of our bodies in interaction with machines (laser cutter and video camera), and what was *not* said or done. I considered these elements together and traced the boundary markings that came to matter in the making of this story. Clearly, focusing primarily on written and spoken words—as is often the traditional focus for researchers of rhetoric and writing—would not give us the whole picture of the dynamic making and boundary-marking processes, either in this moment with Richard or in many more moments over my four years of fieldwork. In this way, I build on the arguments of scholars like Jody Shipka (2011), who exhorts researchers to "trace the highly distributed processes" of meaning making across modalities and to resist "text-dependent conceptions of multimodality by foregrounding the variety of tools, participants, and actions that supported (or may have even thwarted) the production of a particular text" (51–52). Therefore, attending to boundary-marking processes in acts of making demands a dimensional, relational account of rhetorical work—in words, objects, movements, bodies, and images.

In accounts of my in-progress work during the early years of this study, I have described my process of recording and analyzing acts of making (with and without researcher-point-of-view video) as 3D interviewing (Shivers-McNair 2017, 2019). The phrase plays on both the name and the movements of common makerspace fabrication technologies like 3D printers, which move in three dimensions and take their instructions from G code. G code is a series of XYZ coordinates to map and sequence those machine movements in space and time. The phrase is also inspired by the dimensional movements of humans interacting with those fabrication machines, the dimensionality of the objects they produced, and the dimensionality of the meanings and relations that intersected those interactions and objects.

As a story-recording and story-making technique, I found that mobile video can be useful for orienting others—particularly those not familiar with makerspaces—to the multidimensionality of the acts of making I study and to my own dimensionality as a researcher. In this way, I follow a tradition of moving-camera techniques from sensory anthropology and mobile ethnography, like walking with video (Pink 2015) and mobile head-cam video (Laurier 2014). But, as researchers in these traditions are careful to point out, I do not assume that my video camera is capturing a naturally occurring reality, nor that it replaces other forms of description. Rather, its physical presence and my selections (when to switch on and off, whether to select a wide or narrow angle, where to aim the camera, what to get in the frame) are actively shaping and reshaping stories, including what people say and do, as well as what gets presented to audiences of my work.

And while I do my best to keep the camera steady, attend to lighting, and frame shots in ways that are legible, I do not consider myself as a documentary or anthropological filmmaker. While digital video was often important to my work of 3D interviewing (both in terms of data collection and data representation and visualization), I am one researcher, working without a budget for a film crew or extensive equipment. My approach to 3D interviewing with POV video was responsive to those material facts. And because I was often in a space with large machines and constant move-ment, a stationary camera on a tripod was not a viable option, so I either held or wore a small digital video camera as I moved around the space and interacted with participants. As a result, sometimes the footage can be downright dizzying to watch, like when I'm wearing the camera on my head and nodding, or when I turn quickly. Again, though, the point is not filmmaking, but rather a way of attending to embodiment, including the researcher's embodiment, in the analysis and telling of stories.

Much in the way that stories themselves are active boundary markings that create spaces and meanings, so, too, are story-gathering techniques. For example, I found that the logistics of researcher-held (or worn) video changed how I saw and what I focused on. Because my participants and I were often in motion, I could not put microphones on people (as I would in a seated or stationary interview), and as a result, people's voices competed with machine noise and other voices and sounds on camera. This reenacted my own experience of sometime straining to hear or being unable to hear every word spoken, and it presented the same challenges in creating captions and transcripts for the videos that I experienced trying to take notes on conversations in a noisy environment. In this way, the video recordings dislodge—for better and for worse—the primacy of spoken words in a way that draws attention to other ways of making meaning and other ways of bodily production.

Just as video recording encourages me to account for the co-constituting relations of words, sounds, gestures, and spatial relations, the multiple methods I employed to record 3D interviews encouraged me to account for different and co-constitutive ways of knowledge making. In addition to and more frequently than video recorded on a body-worn camera, I used hand-drawn sketches and handwritten notes, photos and video recorded with my iPhone, photos and video recorded with a DSLR camera, and my own embodied memories, particularly since video recording is not always appropriate (when, for example, participants are discussing or modeling proprietary designs). After recording stories in fieldwork, I often began analyzing and making stories by reviewing photos and/or editing video in Adobe Premiere Pro on my laptop. The act of transcribing the interactions and adjusting sound levels drew my attention to nuances and patterns in the interactions, as well as their connections with other events and themes. As I worked, I also consulted my handwritten and typed notes, as well as other photos and videos, looking for relationships and patterns. These relationships and patterns helped me construct both the video stories (the clips I produce) and the stories into which those videos are woven in this book.

Increasingly over time, analysis was not a solitary process. Processes of analyzing blended into processes of recording and documenting, and vice versa. For example, initially, in framing my approach to interviews and interactions, I was guided by traditions of phenomenological qualitative interviewing, which focus on stories and experiences, and of ethnographic field interviews, which build on the relationships and knowledge over time. I also drew on traditions of think-aloud protocols, in which participants describe or comment on what they are doing while they are doing it, and traditions of artifact-based interviews, in which conversations are prompted by physical artifacts.

My approach to 3D interviewing combines both observation and interview, because I rarely interviewed people in the traditional sense of scheduling a time and place to sit and talk about a particular subject. Instead, I moved and talked with people as they moved and talked and made things. In other words, my approach collapsed material-temporal distinctions between interviewing and participant observations (and observations of participation, for that matter). My observations and interactions were certainly guided by my questions, interests, and theoretical frameworks— which include attending to the ways in which the technologies and making practices in a makerspace make some kinds of making and bodies matter more than others—as well as what I have learned in the makerspace over time. But I rarely prepared a structured interview protocol, instead letting the acts of making themselves and the participants shape the questions I asked. Thus, these stories are not so much elicited as much as they are made in researcher-participant interactions.

Furthermore, as I began analyzing and composing the stories in this book, I also frequently shared with participants follow-up questions, observations I had made, or conclusions I was beginning to draw. I invited their co-analysis and co-interpretation or reinterpretation of my understandings, and I shared drafts of the stories in this book through several different iterations over the years. Periodic member checks, in which a researcher shares data and interpretations with participants (members) to check that the data and interpretations resonate with them, are a standard technique in ethnographic and other qualitative research traditions. But for me, conducting member checks quickly turned into opportunities for what Janet Alsup (2010) calls transformative data analysis through a co-constructing of understanding with study participants, who are also comakers of stories.

Therefore, just as the participant perspectives and stories in this book are multiple, so, too, are my methods for story recording and story making. The scope of the study and fieldwork was dynamic in tandem with the dynamics of the spaces and people with whom I was working, and so it followed that my techniques of gathering and making stories were dynamic in tandem with the dynamics of my relationships with participants. I employed 3D interviewing (with and without researcher POV video) throughout the course of the study and across the spaces I worked in, but I also employed other techniques, particularly in my work with Clarissa San Diego, with whom I collaborated on a variety of projects in academic and professional spaces.

Collaborating with Clarissa taught me to recognize myself more as writing *with* people I met in a makerspace than writing *about* a makerspace. In this way, I follow a tradition of community-engaged research in professional and technical communication that emphasizes co-constructing knowledge with communities (Grabill 2013) through a commitment to flexibility and reflexivity on the part of the researcher (Agboka 2013) and through a commitment to "pursuing questions of mutual interest and sharing power and decision making" (Rose et al. 2017, 215). I seek mutually beneficial relationships that involve sharing authorship of publications and presentations with participants, contributing photographic and textual data for participants to use in their own media, and consulting on communication and pedagogical designs.

My first extended interaction with Clarissa (in 2016) began as one of the most traditional-seeming interviews I conducted in the course of the study. Because we were meeting over Skype and it was our first conversation beyond introductions and pleasantries, I did have questions prepared, though I also knew from my years as a journalist and my years as a researcher to be prepared to be flexible. But by the end of the interview—which had become more a conversation and a brainstorm than an interview—we realized that we shared goals, concerns (particularly about inclusion in the maker movement), and an interest in working together. Within just a couple months of that interview-turned-brainstorming session, we started writing an article together for a special issue of *Technical Communication* on globalizing user experience, and since she was both the subject and the coauthor of the article, our process of data generation, collection, analysis, and presentation became intentionally and productively entangled in ways that exceed traditional structures like interviewing to gather data or coding to analyze data.

With that collaborative relationship established, as Makerologist took shape under Clarissa's leadership in 2017, my role—and therefore my actions—in that space looked different than my role and actions in SoDo Makerspace, where I began as an outsider. While I wanted and tried to be useful in SoDo Makerspace with the stories I recorded, I also often didn't know how to be useful, because I was focused on understanding unfamiliar dynamics, and I had entered the space as a researcher-observer. But with the foundations of time in maker communities and an established collaborative relationship, I was able to participate differently in Makerologist. Clarissa knew she could make strategic use of the stories I was recording and making in words, videos, and pictures. For example, I produced Makerologist meeting minutes from my research notes, and I shared the research photos I took at events with Clarissa and her colleagues for them to use for their own social media, web, and presentation materials.

These relationships and practices over time added yet another dimension to what I had initially conceptualized as 3D interviewing: the comaking of stories as a product not only of the relations among humans and technologies and spaces over time, but also as a product of the dynamics of researcher-participant relationships and perspectives over time. This is why I now prefer to think of the approach as relational knowledge-making. In other words, the stories themselves are multiple and relational and so, too, are the practices for recording and making the stories. In this way, I moved toward what Violet Livingston (2015), modeling queer practices of consent for community research, calls "a recursive understanding of consent over time" (129). Not only is consent recursive, but so, too, are the understandings and interpretations of our experiences that emerge and reemerge over the years, as I have shared and discussed versions of this manuscript with the people featured in it. And this brings us to a final characteristic of stories that I want to highlight in the context of this study.

More Than Human and More Than Linear

In illustrating the relationality of stories, I return to Gabriela Raquel Ríos's (2015) point that Indigenous approaches to relationality recognize that "humans and the environment are in a relationship that is co-constituted and not just interdependent" (64). Such an approach reorients my attention to include not just relations among humans (in this case, between researcher and participant, or among participants), but also relations among humans and the environments and things with which they interact. This approach also helps me understand that both the subjects and the makers of stories in this book are more than human. By this I mean that the stories come from and are about a dynamic, complex array of relations among humans, machines, things, spaces, places, and meanings. Those complex relations actively and iteratively mark the boundaries of "human," "machine," "thing," "space," and "meaning" in ways that have consequences for what matters and who matters, what gets made, by whom, and for whom.

Reorienting to relations as unfolding and more than human also highlights the ways in stories are more than linear. For example, Ríos (2015) models "land-based (or spatial) rather than temporal" meaning making (68). In other words, a linear, chronological model for making and telling stories is only one model. When I focus on unfolding relations, different ways of making and telling stories become possible. I model this, for example, in Chapter 3, as I tell the story of how an infinitely unfolding 3D-printed fidget toy I was given in SoDo Makerspace one day became a way of understanding unfolding relations among humans and spaces in the makerspace. And by tracing a series of stories that revolve around the laser cutter in Chapter 4, I point out the ways in which different relations among humans and among humans and machines marked different boundaries and made different actions and understandings possible.

Crucially, in this book, both the stories themselves and the ways in which they were made are more than linear. Just as my relationships with people, spaces, practices, techniques, and theories are dynamic and unfolding, so, too, are my relationships with stories—and my relationships with the meanings that come to matter in the making and telling of stories. In other words, stories themselves are boundary markings that are active, dynamic, multiple, relational, more than human, and more than linear. Rather than starting with a concept or theoretical frame and then selecting examples from my data to illustrate and support that concept or frame, I start with a "mattering moment" and account for how that moment came to matter, which involves a nonlinear construction of a past, present, and future. As Karen Barad (2007) explains, "The past matters and so does the future, but the past is never left behind, never finished once and for all, and the future is not what will come to be in an unfolding of the present moment; rather the past and future are enfolded participants in matter's iterative becoming" (181). In other words, mattering moments rework linear causality by making not only a present moment, but also a past and a future.

Julie Jung's (2014) framework of systems rhetoric is useful for articulating a nonlinear approach to the making and telling of stories:

> In the context of systems rhetoric, the recursive reciprocity afforded by explanation-description couplings emphasizes that *descriptions do not originate in observations of action*. Rather, descriptions become possible when a phenomenon is recognized as being worth noticing, and, further, explanation is the condition of possibility for recognitions of worth. (n.p.)

The experiences, perspectives, and practices I engage in and beyond a makerspace are indeed in a recursive-reciprocal relationship with the theoretical and methodological frameworks I engage. Conceptual frameworks—like definitions of rhetoric, making, and relationality—helped me recognize and explain stories about acts of making. And acts of making—including the making of stories—helped me assemble and reassemble conceptual frameworks for recognizing and explaining stories.

Reciprocal recursivity between description and explanation happens in the context of dynamic relations among people, spaces, things, and meanings. To return to Tony's soundbite at the beginning of this chapter, the making of a story involves things that are happening (in that case, the making of a video about a new fan) and the researcher's and participant's involvement in the recognition and interpretation of things that are happening (jokes about rhetoric and fabrication, and the delivery of a soundbite). This is why it is important for me to attend not only to experiences, practices, perspectives, and frameworks in stories, but also to the dynamics of making stories. Indeed, one of the challenges of this project was developing a method for analyzing, presenting, and discussing stories in a way that accounted for the dynamics of making stories. In other words, I needed a way to account for not only the existence and meanings of stories and relations, but also for the ever-changing dynamics by which stories and relations were made—particularly in a study that spans four years.

As a result, the stories in this book were made and remade in many iterations over several years in an arc that resembles the iterative practices of prototyping I observed in and beyond a makerspace. Before I spent time in a makerspace, I had not thought of writing in terms of prototyping, but I was struck by how Alex Cheker, owner of MyOpen3D, described his making process: "The most important thing [my mentor] taught me was that you build the first prototype fast and with whatever you have. You see if you can get it to work, and you learn from it. It's almost never going to work exactly the way you want anyway. Then, if it works, you spend time on version two." Alex's words resonated with my own writing practices and with the way I teach writing. Thinking of my writing as prototyping became a way for me to identify with people in a makerspace as I made and remade stories about making.

Thinking of writing as prototyping also helped me overcome the overwhelming (but familiar) block of where to begin. Consider, for example, my first story prototype for this book, which began with the video of Richard and the laser cutter in Figure 3. Why this particular moment? Why start with the moment of Richard's fingers' close encounter with a laser? Quite simply, this moment had been on my mind: initially because it was a surprising moment, but also because I had spent many hours with the video footage as I learned a new-to-me video-editing program (Adobe Premiere Pro). I had first edited the clip as part of a methods-focused video designed to illustrate what a 3D interview looks like. But editing the video got me thinking even more about the ways in which a laser passing near Richard's fingers mattered—for me, for him, for the laser cutter, for an understanding of making.

Richard's interaction with the laser cutter became a mattering moment: a moment that has come to matter in both a physical sense (involving the making/remaking of objects, affect, bodies) and a discursive sense (involving the making/remaking of knowledge, recognition, theory). The story does not matter in an absolute or inherent sense. The story matters in a relational sense: it came to matter through relations of experiences, perspectives, practices, theories, and methodologies. Like all the stories in this book, this story could have been told in different ways. Different things could have been included and excluded, and different things could come to matter. The story is inseparable from the dynamics of its making. And a prototyping approach helps me remember that the process of telling stories about mattering moments is iterative and negotiated.

Therefore, the process of moving forward with creating the stories in this book was like disassembling a first-version prototype and sifting through the parts for what worked, what cut could be fixed, what was missing, and what could be set aside. These decisions were informed not only by my own evolving sense, but from the feedback and perspectives of participants, mentors, and anonymous readers of earlier versions of this book. From disassembled components and unfolding relations, I assembled new story prototypes. Thus, the stories I construct are not meant to recount a sequence of linear-causal events that led to a moment in time; rather, the making of stories reworks causality—making not only a present moment (the telling of a story), but also a past (what the story is about and how it came to matter) and a future (new possible understandings, relations, and stories). As I illustrated in my discussion of interacting with Richard while he operated the laser cutter, when I inhabit and revisit a story, things I have heard and seen and learned in the past that might have seemed unconnected or even inconsequential at the time come into sharp focus. And a possible future emerges that includes possibilities for action, telling stories and asking more questions, and an emergent sense of the material-discursive practices and concepts.

Stories like the ones in this book are what Barad (2007) calls apparatuses that "produce differences that matter—they are boundary-marking practices that are formative of matter and meaning, productive of, and part of, the phenomena produced" (146). Instead of attempting to reflect or reconstruct a preexisting reality, I am actively creating, cocreating, and recreating stories, realities, and relations. The videos that accompany these stories throughout the book invite readers to relate to the people, machines, and spaces in the story while also drawing attention to the making of the stories, particularly through the camera's movements and perspectives. The stories are about and are themselves dynamic relations and boundary markings among people, machines, things, ideas, spaces, and acts of making over time. It is impossible to fully account for these ongoing, dynamic complexities, but the stories in this book take up the challenge of multidimensional relationality.

CHAPTER THREE

Spatial Manipulations

On a Friday in February 2016, I opened the gray metal door to SoDo Makerspace and found Tony Loiseleur (lead blog writer and shop assistant at the time) at his workspace in front of the 3D printers. I headed toward him, fieldwork notebook in hand, hoping to talk to him about his work in the space and my interpretations of previous observations and conversations. Tony greeted me, and then to my surprise he said, "OK, put down your notebook."

I blinked. "What?"

"No, really, you can do it!" Tony teased. "Set it down right here." He pointed to a spot on his desk.

"OK," I said, still unsure what was going on.

"Here, hold this." Tony put a small white plastic object comprised of small, interconnected discs in my hands.

"What is it?" I asked.

"Just try turning it inside out," he said. I did, and suddenly I was hooked, because the toy turns inside out infinitely (Figure 4). I was delighted at first by the surprise of it and then by the act of turning it inside out over and over. That surprise and delight registered on my face, to which Tony responded, "Pretty great, huh?"

This wasn't the first time I'd encountered a surprising 3D-printed object in the makerspace: I'd held a prosthetic hand, a collapsible birdhouse, and a plastic vase that looked like glass—just to name a few. But the endless inside-out motion of manipulating this object was weirdly addicting, more so than anything else I'd encountered. I reluctantly set it down, eventually, to put on my head-mounted camera and pick up my notebook. I asked Tony

Figure 4. 3D-printed spatial manipulation toy, photographed by
Daniel M. McNair

again what the thing was called, and he demurred again. "I don't know; I'm
not sure if it has a name. I just found it on Thingiverse." (Thingiverse is
a website run by MakerBot, a mass-market manufacturer of 3D printers,
where people upload and download open-source stereo lithographic [.stl]
files for 3D printing.)

Concerned about how I would describe this object in writing, I pressed:
"What was the file named on Thingiverse?" Tony didn't remember—and
he didn't think it mattered for introducing the object to people. After all,
as he said when he described sharing the object with his wife, "You don't
have to *say* [what it is] so much as just *show*." Later that day, though, when
Tony started making another of these objects, he found the Thingiverse

file again and told me it was called a "spatial manipulation toy." This time, I observed his printing process from start to finish, and I left that evening with my very own spatial manipulation toy, which I played with nonstop on my walk and bus ride home.

This chapter begins with this story because the infinitely unfolding motion of this fidget toy became a way for me to understand and visualize unfolding relations in SoDo Makerspace as I was beginning to tell the stories in this book. This story and the stories in this chapter are an account of many unfolding spatial manipulations. Using the name of the fidget toy to describe these relations highlights the interplay of the toy itself, the name *spatial manipulations*, and the definitions of rhetoric that I draw upon. The spatial manipulations of the fidget toy's movements when I play with it remind me of Candice Rai's (2016) description of rhetoric as "a force that not only orders our lives but also animates our bodies. Gets under our skin. Puts things into motion through and beyond human will. Emerging from and wedded to the co-constitutive interactions of language, people, things, matter, and all other presences and forces in the world" (7). Additionally, as a metaphor for relations in SoDo Makerspace, *spatial manipulations* reminds me to attend to what rhetorical forces (emerging from relations) put into motion: from small-scale spatial manipulations, like the weird appeal of a simple toy, to large-scale spatial manipulations, like the ways in which makers (human and nonhuman) make space for themselves and their makings over time. And as a way of understanding the making of these stories, *spatial manipulations* highlights the ways in which story making and storytelling are themselves acts of creating and sharing space, to echo Malea Powell's (2012) definition of a story as "an event in which I try to hold some of the complex shimmering strands of a constellative, epistemological space long enough to share them with you" (384).

The week after I was introduced to the spatial manipulation toy, I confessed to Tony that when I was trying to write about the spatial manipulation toy, I wanted to play with it instead. "I don't know what it is about [the toy], but it tickles some part of our animal brain," Tony replied, noting that it had been a big hit all week with visitors in SoDo Makerspace. I told him I'd also found myself playing with it while I paced around my apartment trying to sort out the stories in this chapter in my mind. "Yeah, well, you know they say for writing: when you're stuck, take a walk. This is just taking it to the next level," he said. Perhaps this is why the toy continues to draw me in, even after the initial surprise of the toy's kaleidoscope-like movements wore off. More so than any 3D-printed object I'd encountered in makerspaces thus far (including my own attempt to 3D-print an object), this one insinuated itself into my daily movements and altered my daily movements. Or, to borrow Candice Rai's (2016) words, it got under my skin.

As Richard Albritton (featured in the Figure 3 video in the previous chapter at https://doi.org/10.3998/mpub.11724511.cmp5) explained to me once, the collection of 3D-printed objects, including the spatial manipulation toy, in SoDo Makerspace often helped people understand what is possible to print. And knowing what is possible to print is certainly an important (and perhaps the first) step in learning how and what to print. In this way, the toy is an example of what David Sheridan (2010) calls fabricated rhetoric, a 3D object with persuasive power. It commanded my attention, and like many other fabricated objects displayed in SoDo Makerspace for visitors, it also negotiated and localized information about what "making" looked like there—to echo Angela Haas's (2012) definition of rhetoric as "the negotiation of cultural information—and its historical, social, economic, and political influences—to affect social action (persuade)" (287).

For Tony, the spatial manipulation toy was just one step—however enthralling—in a process of learning 3D printers well enough to operate them independently and teach certification classes. In 2016, Tony was learning how to operate 3D printers designed and owned by Alex Cheker (MyOpen3D), who was at the time operating some of his 3D printers at SoDo Makerspace (in addition to his own workspaces). And while the printing of this toy was Tony's first time to operate Alex's 3D printers, he had printed objects on the MakerBot printers (which, until early 2016, were the only working 3D printers in SoDo Makerspace) and had also worked on the laser cutter and CNC.

Alex's instructions to Tony were not to print a specific file, but rather to keep finding and printing things until he used up at least a spool of 3D printer filament. "When you're done going through a spool or two, I'll show you the advanced stuff," Alex told him that day, as they prepared the second spatial manipulation toy file for printing. While the printing of the toy was a step in a process, it had its own significance for Tony. As he explained to me, he wanted to make something for people to play with when they entered the makerspace and felt nervous or uncertain. And because his wife liked the spatial manipulation toy when he had showed it to her, his next 3D printing project was a gift for her: a set of interlocking, seahorse-shaped gears that, like the spatial manipulation toy, can be turned endlessly.

Making Makers

I came to understand that there were many spatial manipulations threaded through the phenomenon of making a maker in SoDo Makerspace. One of these spatial manipulations was recognizing oneself and being recognized by others as a maker—particularly by "going from idea to object," as CEO Eric Renn often emphasized. Eric also identified the delight of seeing an idea turn into an object as an important way of engaging with visitors to the makerspace. For example, in July 2015, I observed Eric engaging a group of young men from the Seattle Youth Employment Program (SYEP) (most of whom, he told me, were African immigrants) in a conversation about making in the makerspace. They were all standing around the table with the 3D printers and a collection of 3D-printed objects as Eric told them stories of what people make using machines like 3D printers, laser cutters, sewing machines, and CNC machines. They picked up and played with the objects as Eric talked, and they often seemed more interested in the objects than in what he was saying. He even got them to brainstorm a list of things they could imagine making or might want to make and wrote their list on the whiteboard by the table: the list included clothing items, jewelry, phone cases, a bow and arrow, and a display case for boxing gloves. But Eric soon moved the group over to the laser cutter to watch an idea turn into an object: specifically, he asked them all to type their first name or nickname and choose a font for it in the design program on the computer connected to the laser cutter, and then they watched as the laser etched their names into blocks of plywood, which it then cut out into separate pieces.

Eric later explained to me that he chose the laser cutter because "it goes so quickly from idea to object" (compared to, say, a 3D printer, which can take hours to print even a small object like the spatial manipulation toy). He chose to have the youth cut out their names because he believes that the ability to personalize things is an important part of being a maker. In fact, this was one of the first things he told me on my first visit to SoDo Makerspace, and it's a common practice in his own use of the laser cutter: for example, I watched him engrave his name on a leather passport cover his wife gave him in anticipation of their family trip to Germany in December 2015. And, indeed, the young men were visibly more engaged by the personalized name etchings than they were with the table of already-made objects and the list of possibilities on the board. Still, though, as I myself have experienced, watching someone else cut out something you personalized on the laser cutter does not a laser cutter operator make. What's more, after the initial surprise or curiosity of watching a machine operate for the first time wears off, fabrication machines are not especially exciting to watch. The laser cutter, at least, works quickly compared to the 3D printers and CNC mill.

For many of the SYEP group, this was to be their only interaction with the laser cutter. One young man stayed behind after their volunteer shift was over because he had an idea for the laser cutter. He asked Tony, who was helping Eric supervise the group that day, about cutting out a plywood pendant in the shape of Africa with a heart over his home country, so he could hang it on a necklace, and Tony helped him make the idea into an object. Others in the group were interested in this idea, too, and Tony showed me one of the pendants the following week. More than two years later, in a reflection written and shared with several others of the Makerologist team (many of whom are SoDo Makerspace alumni), Tony returned to that moment with the young man who stayed behind:

> He decided on making wood jewelry for his friends and family that reflected his Somali heritage. Under his aesthetic direction, I helped him locate designs online and showed him how to render them in a CAD [computer-aided design] program, and then showed him how to have those designs etched and cut on the laser cutter. I thought it would end there, as generally, I've seen how happy most people are when they walk into a makerspace with an idea, then leave with their idea in physical form afterward. But then he said something that stuck with me since: "Y'know, I could go into business making this kind of stuff. This could be my job." He smiled then, which was the first time I'd ever seen him that happy and engaged during that entire summer program.

I did not interview the young men (because they were minors, and because the nature of their relationship to SoDo Makerspace would have made it difficult to obtain guardian consent for interviews), so I do not know how those experiences with the laser cutter changed or did not change their relationship with 3D fabrication technologies. To my knowledge, though, none of the SYEP volunteers returned to SoDo Makerspace. I can imagine that without regular access to these large, expensive technologies, thinking of oneself as a maker of laser-cut or CNC-milled things might not be a priority or even a possibility.

Making Space

For Tony, printing the spatial manipulation toy was, in many ways, a microcosm of a larger spatial manipulation: making space for himself in SoDo Makerspace (in both a physical and metaphorical sense). Marking oneself as a maker involves not only skills and knowledge, or even simply an affinity for maker culture, but also physical space, relationships with people and machines, time, and socioeconomic realities. Tony, whose prior training and experience is in professional writing, explained that being a "regular" in SoDo Makerspace meant being, in his words, "basically a shop intern" who was not paid as he learned the machines and helped with daily operations. Because SoDo Makerspace never operated on a model of having paid employees, the only way people like Tony could be involved in the space, at least in the early years, was as a volunteer.

In late 2014, after SoDo Makerspace first opened its doors, Clarissa recruited volunteers in a system that exchanged volunteer hours for free time on the machines. Following Clarissa's recommendation, SoDo Makerspace initially implemented an à la carte pricing structure in which, instead of paying for monthly memberships, people pay for time on the machines or for someone else to operate the machine for them. Volunteers and partners came in and out of SoDo Makerspace over the years. Eventually, volunteers (like Tony) and partners (like Alex, who operated some of his 3D printers there in 2016) could share in profits from conducting certifications or working on client-commissioned projects. In its last year of operations, SoDo Makerspace operated on a paid membership model.

When Tony connected with SoDo Makerspace in June 2015, none of the original volunteers that Clarissa had recruited were still there (to my knowledge), and his vision was to stick out that initial "internship" period to position himself to eventually become a paid employee. For the first several months, he worked more on educational outreach: for example, he helped lead the SYEP groups over the summer of 2015, and during the fall, he was often at various locations outside SoDo Makerspace helping teach fabrication workshops for children. Tony decided to move back to the production work of SoDo Makerspace in early 2016. By then, Alex had brought his professional-grade 3D printers and his expertise as the "resident 3D printing genius" (as Eric referred to him), which meant Tony could become a 3D printer operator and share in profits from that work.

Tony's tenacity in making space for himself in SoDo Makerspace is evident not only in his willingness to stick out the "internship" for months, but also in his work to secure a physical workspace for himself in a room where furniture is constantly on the move and workspace is premium real estate. One constant in SoDo Makerspace was that regardless of whether or not the regulars had a dedicated desk/workspace, they moved around the space—to machines and to other people's workspaces—often. And even when they were at their own spaces, they were often still talking to each other, or at least jumping in and out of conversations. Eric moved around the most, perhaps not surprisingly, given his role. In the spring and summer of 2015, the back half of SoDo Makerspace was cluttered with tools, donated equipment, and extra furniture, and so Richard set up his equipment and projects on one of the work tables.

As more people became regulars in SoDo Makerspace, they claimed the back half of the space for their work areas, since Eric wanted to keep at least the front half open for meetings and trainings. In fact, by January 2016, Alex (who also worked from home and from his own workshop) and Eric were the only regulars who did not have permanent desks in SoDo Makerspace: they both worked at the conference table in the front half of the space. Eric told me many times that he wished that there were no permanent desks. "That's not the ethos I want," he explained once. "I want it to be where at the end of the day, everyone packs up their stuff and stores it or takes it home." This is, in fact, what Eric did every day, but Eric's self-described role as "the facilitator" was different from the roles of the other regulars, who were also designing their own products and carrying out jobs for clients. For the other regulars, having a workspace mattered, and it certainly mattered for Tony. When he first returned to SoDo Makerspace in fall 2015 to focus on becoming a shop assistant, Tony had to negotiate space for himself.

In summer 2015, Tony had a box with his name written on it and a chair next to Richard's desk, but he didn't have a dedicated place to set up his laptop. In fall 2015, Tony used another regular's desk while he was away, but he soon had to move in anticipation of his colleague's return. In winter 2016, one of Tony's colleagues finally helped him build a small desk from scrap materials, which he placed in front of the new 3D printing station, where he was apprenticing with Alex. But this location was short-lived, because both Eric and Alex objected to Tony's desk being in the way of the 3D-printing machines. Finally, in early spring 2016, a shuffling of desks among the other regulars (who had for several months taken up residence in one of the back quadrants of the space) opened up a spot for Tony, who promptly took it.

Being near Richard had been Tony's goal since his return to the main space in late 2015. "I wanted to be near him so I could just be like"—he mimed leaning across a desk—"'Hey, Rich! What about this?'" I realized, in the process of telling this story, that while Tony's original goal, as he had explained it to me and as he had explained in his first blog post, was to get "maker skills" (which he imagined as primarily learning technologies and techniques), that goal had morphed into integrating himself (physically and relationally) into the distributed knowledge network of the space. I realized that Tony's work making himself into being recognized as a maker in SoDo Makerspace, like my own work making myself into a researcher in SoDo Makerspace, is as much about integration into a dynamic, distributed network (of humans, machines, objects, and cyborg combinations of these) as it is about individually integrating skills or transferring individual knowledge across contexts or machines. At the same time, Tony did in fact begin sharing in profits from the machine certification trainings he conducted and from the client jobs to which he contributed, while continuing to produce and edit social media and other internal and external communications in SoDo Makerspace, from technical instructions to client emails.

Tony maintained his desk location in SoDo Makerspace through the end of 2016, after which point he and Alex left SoDo Makerspace to dedicate their time to the MyOpen3D workshop (located, at the time, in Seattle's Central District). Tony worked from the MyOpen3D workshop during 2017, and in 2018 he moved to the Makerologist office in Impact Hub Seattle. Meanwhile, in SoDo Makerspace, configurations of people, workspaces, machines, and materials continued to move around the space throughout its life span. In fact, the laser cutter was one of the only things that did *not* move until SoDo Makerspace closed in 2018. It now resides at the West Seattle Tool Library, led by Micah Summers, who was a cofounder of SoDo Makerspace and a Makerologist team member.

Tony's spatial-temporal trajectory of relations in SoDo Makerspace taught me that despite the name *makerspace*, neither space nor maker is a given, but is negotiated continually and differently for different bodies. Indeed, Tony's trajectory of making space also inspired me to attend to my own trajectory of making space. This chapter is comprised of mattering moments, or stories that came to matter as a result of the relations of my participation in spaces, conversations with people, theoretical engagements, and ongoing analysis. As Karen Barad (2007) explains, "The past matters and so does the future, but the past is never left behind, never finished once and for all, and the future is not what will come to be in an unfolding of the present moment; rather the past and future are enfolded participants in matter's iterative becoming" (181). This story of Tony's making space for himself is a past that unfolded in my meditations on and conversations with him about the spatial manipulation toy.

Specifically, this story came to matter for me through the relations of maker movement rhetorics, shared experiences, and conceptual lenses. I came to this study aware that the maker movement is often associated with the promise of democratizing access to fabrication technologies, and Tony's story of becoming a 3D printer operator nuances my understanding of that promise. His is a story of access, but that access did not happen overnight. It involved precarity, self-advocacy, and tenacity over time. Thus, while makerspaces can democratize access to technologies, access is not simply a matter of making machines available. As Adam Banks (2006) argues, material access is only the beginning, while "transformative access" to technology involves meaningful inclusion in the ongoing development and administration of a technology (45).

This story also came to matter because I identified with Tony's background as a writer, ethnographer, and maker "newb," and with his determination to make space for himself. I was initially intimidated by the people and machines in the space, as someone without prior experience in the technologies in the makerspace, and as someone who was often the only woman-identified person in the space. It took months for me to learn about and build relationships with the machines and processes and people in the makerspace. And through the conceptual lens of Natasha Jones, Kristen Moore, and Rebecca Walton's (2016) 3Ps (attending to positionality, privilege, and power), I recognize that the intersections of my identities— particularly my whiteness, nondisabled status, and socioeconomic status as a university-employed researcher—made it possible for me to negotiate the boundary marks of gender difference and technical knowledge difference in the ways that I did.

Saying and Showing

In making and telling these stories, I have come to understand that the experience of making the spatial manipulation toy with Tony was entangled in many spatial manipulations—the immensely complex entanglement of bodies, ideas, identities, knowledges, and machine movements involved in making makers, things, and space over time. I return to my conversation with Tony about the name of the spatial manipulation toy to examine another dimension of spatial manipulations: the relationship between saying and showing, to use Tony's words. As Tony said of the spatial manipulation toy, "You don't have to *say* [what it is] so much as just *show*." This is true in the making of this chapter, too: for example, I chose to make a GIF of my hands moving the spatial manipulation toy to begin this chapter, because that GIF explains the movement more succinctly than I could in words for readers who can access visual content. And because I cannot assume universal access to visual content, I still used words to describe the toy in my account of my interaction with Tony, in addition to providing alt text for the digital image. And still, neither that GIF nor its alt text is the same as playing with the spatial manipulation toy, feeling the plastic and the gentle grating of the surfaces against each other as it turns endlessly inside out.

Just as visual content joins alphabetic text in this book as a way of both saying and showing spatial manipulations, combinations of words and movements functioned as ways of saying and showing in the makerspace, both in human relations and in human-machine relations. For example, G code (the language that the laser cutter, 3D printers, and CNC machines use to carry out jobs) translates human-designed digital shapes into machine movements on XYZ axes. Alex explained this the day I observed his mentoring Tony on the second printing of the spatial manipulation toy. Tony had just initiated the slicing process in a program called Slic3r, and I asked what that meant.

"Slicing is the process of taking a three-dimensional shape and turning it into G code, which is the instructions—line-per-line instructions—that tell the printer how to move and push plastic out, what temperature to set itself at, and all that," Alex explained. "It's basically taking a shape"—he mimed holding a 3D shape in his left hand—"and turning it into instructions"—he mimed holding the same shape in his right hand—"on how to reproduce that shape." What struck me about this interaction, as with many others I've participated in, was not the primacy of either gesture or verbal language but, in fact, the relations of several languages (spoken and written English, shapes on screens, G code, and the many languages of programmed machine and body circuits) and several gestures (human and nonhuman). These relations resulted in many spatial manipulations—including the spatial manipulation toy, Tony's ongoing learning process and relationship to SoDo Makerspace, and, eventually, these stories themselves.

Consider, for example, the many dimensions of relations in this particular interaction. Alex verbally instructed Tony to reslice the file, since they had adjusted the print settings. Tony instructed Slic3r, via clicks of a computer mouse, to transform the shapes of the spatial manipulation toy file (as well as the settings he specified for infill (the density of the object), perimeter layers (which create a solid surface over the honeycomb pattern of the infill/interior), and the temperature for the 3D printer's extruder (which melts the plastic filament much like a hot glue gun melts a stick of glue). Having seen and heard this, I verbally asked about slicing, to which Alex responded using both words and gestures. I, in turn, mentally connected his explanation to my prior knowledge of how G code works. Once Slic3r finished, it sent the G code to Alex's Prusa I3+ printer, which then translated the G code into movements to make the discs of the spatial manipulation toy.

Once the printer finished, Tony followed Alex's instructions for removing the clear glass printing surface from the red bed (using a fingernail and a spatula), and then he set the glass on the gray shelf surface to cool. (The printer bed is heated to keep the filament from cooling too quickly and solidifying on contact.) As the cool surface of the shelf cooled the glass, the glass began to shrink and pull away from the 3D-printed pieces, making what Alex described as "tiny snap-crackle-pop sounds" that can only be heard in very close proximity, which Tony and Alex invited me to experience for myself, and I did. The sounds were indeed very faint, but audible with my ear nearly touching the glass.

Once the tiny snap-crackle-pop sounds had ceased, Tony picked up the glass and tilted it to let the pieces slide off, and most did immediately. He nudged a still-stuck piece off gently. While we waited for these green discs to print, Tony had disassembled the first spatial manipulation toy made from white discs. Tony handed me three white discs and three green discs, keeping the remaining six green and white discs, and he instructed me to snap the pieces together, alternating colors, then snap the two ends of the chain together. The result was two green and white spatial manipulation toys (one to stay in the space, and one that Tony gave to me, pictured in the video that begins this chapter). [link in digital version]

While Tony is absolutely right that sometimes it is more effective to show than to say, sometimes saying and naming are more expedient than showing or doing. For example, Tony could presumably have eventually figured out all that he needed to know about printing on the Prusa I3+ by tinkering and troubleshooting—and indeed, Alex prescribed at least a spool's worth of printing and tinkering to give Tony the opportunity to figure out things for himself. But Alex also saved Tony quite a lot of tinkering time by giving him verbal explanations and advice. And Tony, a writer by training, told me about a month before this interaction that he thought stories could play a powerful role in helping people connect with SoDo Makerspace. "I see people come in the space because they saw it online and are curious, but they just kind of stand there or wander around confused until Richard or Eric goes up to them like, 'Hey, can I help you?' and they still don't really know [what they want to make]," he said. Tony's comment resonated strongly with my memory of my own first visit to SoDo Makerspace.

Tony was convinced that the solution to this problem is storytelling: not only stories of making things on various machines, but also stories of how makers are made. "Eric wants me to blog [on the SoDo Makerspace website] about stuff happening in the makerspace, and that's fine, I can do that, but I think people need to see those narratives [of how makers themselves are made] to really get it," he explained. Tony's attention to the importance of stories echoes Malea Powell's (2012) argument that stories are doing the complex, constellating work of letting us enter and share a space (384).

And often making things and making makers involves a combination of saying and showing, as in the case of the 3D printer certification materials developed by Alex. In February 2016, Alex wrote a manual for 3D printer certification training that includes common terminology and definitions, pictures, safety protocols, step-by-step instructions, and troubleshooting tips. Tony, who copyedited the manual, offered me a copy, noting that it was the first written certification manual in SoDo Makerspace, and that he hoped it would be a model for certification manuals for the other machines. As I read the manual, I drew on my experiences observing people working with 3D printers—and especially Alex's training Tony the day he made the spatial manipulation toys—to understand the instructions, and I realized that the instructions didn't make reference to the settings for infill, perimeters, and top and bottom layers that I'd heard Alex and Tony discussing.

The next time I saw Alex, I asked him if those particular settings were perhaps too project-specific to include in the manual, and he replied, "Well, they're not in this version, but they should probably be in the next version. But actually, I also made these"—he reached for a set of three 3D-printed tabs on a key chain and offered them to me—"for the three standard settings." On one side, each tab (one labeled "lite," one "medium," one "strong") included settings for infill, perimeter, and top and bottom layer printed on a sticker label (Figure 5). And each tab was printed with the set-

Figure 5. 3D-printing instructions in written text and in labeled objects

tings described on the label, allowing a user to compare setting configurations by seeing and touching. I remarked to Alex that, for me, the tabs were a far more effective way to teach and model the settings than just a written description or even a picture. In this way, as practitioners and teachers of technical communication well know, "saying" and "showing" worked together for effective instructions, just as "saying" and "showing" intertwine in the rhetorical work of spatial manipulations—making makers, making things, or making space for ourselves or others.

But making space is an ongoing negotiation—both for me as a researcher and for the people and things in SoDo Makerspace. For example, neither Tony nor I would claim that, by summer 2016, the boundary-marking relations through which his skills as a writer were considered separate from (and less valuable than) his making skills had been entirely overcome. That summer, I watched Tony operating the sewing machine with ease while he commented that other people in the space were "more useful" in terms of fabrication skills, but that he did feel he contributed to the space in more ways than just social media content, now that he could operate the machines himself. Just as he learned several martial arts traditions to become a "full-spectrum warrior," Tony explained, by adding fabrication skills to his writing skills he became a "full-spectrum creator." He went on to point out that beyond the content production and editing he does and even his work with the fabrication technologies, he understood his ability to explain those technologies and their possibilities to newcomers in SoDo Makerspace as an important contribution.

"For places like this to grow and expand, there has to be someone there not just to advertise it but to *explain* it to people," he said. "When we have people walk in because they've heard of makerspaces or 3D printing, it's important to help them wrap their minds around what it means for them and their communities that they have access to these technologies." In other words, to do the rhetorical work of negotiating and localizing information about making and of creating opportunities for visitors to identify with the kinds of making in SoDo Makerspace, one needed to be, in Tony's words, a full-spectrum creator. Tony's metaphor resonates with the words of computers and composition scholar Cynthia Selfe (2009), who argues that writing teachers should teach multiple modalities of communication because students "need a full quiver of semiotic modes from which to select" in order to engage in "wickedly complex communicative tasks" (645). I have found this to be true in my own writing about SoDo Makerspace and making, and I have found it to be true in how I approach the teaching of writing.

As both a researcher and a teacher, I am less interested in calling everything "writing" or "rhetoric" than I am in examining writing and rhetoric as forms of and in relationship to other forms of making. This means recognizing the entanglement of saying and showing, of languages and gestures—as well as the differential processes by which "saying" and "showing" are recognized as such—as part of the processes of spatial manipulations. In other words, making and manipulating space involves meaning-making with words, bodies, objects, and interactions, and these different ways of making meaning are marked in relation to each other, and in interactions, just as more or less human/makers and machines and things and connections are made, unmade, and remade. This has implications not only for how we theorize and study rhetoric, writing, and technology design (and other forms of making), but also for how we teach writing and rhetoric.

As Tony explains in the video in Chapter 1 (Figure 2, at https://doi .org/10.3998/mpub.11724511.cmp3), the tools and technologies we make are extensions of human capability—including, I would add, our capacity for making meanings. A more than human but still human-centered approach to technology design means thinking about design and making in this way, because such an approach foregrounds the making and remaking of bodies—and all the possibilities and pitfalls that entails. Indeed, the relations of human bodies and nonhuman things in these stories resonates with the work Jacqueline Rhodes and Jonathan Alexander (2015) do in their multimodal webtext *Techne: Queer Meditations on Writing the Self* to emphasize the phenomenological, queer/ing interactions of bodies and things:

> As we touch our technology, we are increasingly reminded of how it touches us back, sometimes through the agency of others reaching out to us. . . . What happens to us as we feel ourselves touched by our technologies? [Sara] Ahmed [in *Queer Phenomenology*, 2006] argues that bodies are "shaped by contact with objects and with others, with 'what' is near enough to be reached. Bodies may even take shape through such contact, or take the shape of that contact. What gets near is both shaped by what bodies do, which in turn affects what bodies can do." ("Orientations")

These co-constituting relations happen on many levels of spatial manipulation (or orientation, to use Ahmed's word)—not only in touch and gesture but also in language.

Given these co-constituting relations, we must attend to the relational and differential processes by which objects become objects, rhetoric becomes rhetoric, actions become actions, and humans become more or less human, or more or less maker. Making involves complex, unfolding relations through what Barad (2007) describes as intra-actions that "materialize different phenomena—different marks on bodies," and therefore "contribute to the differential mattering of the world" (178). In other words, to study the relations of saying and showing, of humans and nonhumans, we need accounts of how boundaries are iteratively marked—for instance, the boundaries of maker, technologies, writing, and space—in particular configurations of space and time. After all, Sharon Crowley (1999) reminds us that "distinctions and boundaries are never disinterested," and studying the partisan nature of boundaries has long been the project of rhetorical studies (363). Despite the promises and hopes of democratizing access in the contemporary maker movement, "making" is not inherently or universally accessible, inclusive, or empowering. Rather, making—and being recognized as a maker—is situated in specific relations of bodies, cultures, materials, and spaces. When some practices are marked as "making" more than others, some bodies can more easily be marked as "makers" than others.

Furthermore, intervening in a material-rhetorical situation ourselves—or teaching our students to intervene in material-rhetorical situations—involves all of our body in the making, not just our mind and linguistic communications. Alex's approach to training Tony on his 3D printers involved a combination of several ways of making meaning: direct instruction (like "Go ahead and re-slice that file since you've made changes to the settings, because any time you make changes, you should reslice"); answering Tony's questions directly (or turning them back on Tony for him to figure out himself: "You tell me what the perimeter values correspond to"); engaging with Tony in recounting and considering mistakes, problems, and successes; watching Tony go through steps, doing some of the steps with or for him, leaving him alone to work on his own; and prescribing a lot of time (measured in spools of filament used, not in objects completed) to "make mistakes," "break things (and don't worry about it, because you know I can fix it)," and "learn to eyeball" things that initially require measuring. But Tony's training also involved drawing on their relationship as colleagues, in the form of friendly chatting during down time (of which there was plenty in a print job that took about an hour and twenty minutes) about shared interests (music and gaming) and about happenings in the makerspace. And the training also involved Tony's determination to make space for himself in SoDo Makerspace.

These layers of relations resonate with Shaun Slattery's concept of mediation as a technical communication practice, specifically, "the use of existing documents, notes, and software necessary to 'do' technical communication" (354). Slattery offers mediation as a way of bridging the divide (in the literature on teaching technical communication, if not in the professional practice of technical communication) between what he categorizes as tool-based skills and higher-order competencies (or rhetorical skills). In other words, Slattery's concept of mediation undercuts the assumption that rhetorical skills are separate from technological skills, and as Laura Gonzales (2018a) argues, rhetorical skills like translation *are* technological skills.

In this way, work like Slattery's and Gonzales's helps us understand the co-constituting relations of rhetorics, technologies, materials, and bodies involved in Tony's training on the 3D printer. But such a view of teaching and doing rhetoric means that rhetoric is "wickedly complex," to return to Cynthia Selfe's (2009) words (645). And those wickedly complex relations involve not only making things (and relations), but also breaking things (and relations).

CHAPTER FOUR

Disequilibrium

"Just a little fire in the laser cutter." This is not a sentence I would have anticipated uttering before my involvement in a makerspace. But one morning in February 2016, when one of the regulars walked in and looked mildly surprised to see Eric Renn, CEO of SoDo Makerspace, sweeping debris out of the base of the machine, I said to him, by way of explanation, "Just a little fire in the laser cutter," while snapping pictures with my phone and jotting down notes. And just like that, we all went about our business. This is not to suggest that laser cutter fires are not dangerous—they are—but, rather, that we had all by this point seen fires in the laser cutter and were not particularly surprised. In fact, a portion of this chapter is dedicated to stories of fires in the laser cutter. Just as the story of the spatial manipulation toy (in the previous chapter) came to matter to me as a way of understanding unfolding relations in acts of making, the story of this little laser cutter fire came to matter to me as a way of understanding disequilibrium in making processes in SoDo Makerspace.

Disequilibrium includes human errors and machine malfunctions in the operation of technologies, as well as intentional practices that stretch (or break) shop rules and machine specifications. But disequilibrium also includes imbalances and disruptions in a makerspace-as-system, particularly in social dynamics and tensions between the amateur ethos of the space and systems of production that privilege traditional expertise. To return to Candice Rai's (2016) point that rhetoric "puts things into motion through and beyond human will" (7), instances of disequilibrium like laser cutter fires remind me that those rhetorical motions can be both constructive and destructive (depending on the point of view). Disequilibrium sometimes happens in ways that humans and machines do not intend, but sometimes humans bring about disequilibrium on purpose (or at least don't try terribly hard to avoid it) as a way of innovating in order to do the rhetorical work of solving local and global problems, to echo Donnie Johnson Sackey's (2018) definition of rhetoric as "a means (tactics/tools) whereby people come together to solve localized problems in movement that frequently oscillates between local and global foci" (156).

Furthermore, disequilibrium includes intentionally or knowingly disrupting or destabilizing systems (knowledge, processes, comfort levels, etc.) as a teaching and learning strategy for making in ways that resonate with what Marc Santos and Megan McIntyre (2016) describe in their approach to a disequilibrating technical communication pedagogy. Many of the people I have observed allow for and even cultivate a relatively high tolerance for disequilibrium as a practice of rhetorical invention, in the forms of troubleshooting, failing fast, and a "ready, fire, aim" philosophy (as Eric describes it). Observing strategic uses of disequilibrium influenced me to create more space for disequilibrium not only in my own practices of making (including writing), but also in my practice of teaching writing.

And experiences of disequilibrium between a human and a machine (intentional or unintentional on the part of the human) are not separate from experiences of disequilibrium among people in a makerspace. For example, the assumptions about human bodies and abilities that are built into many of the fabrication technologies in a makerspace render some bodies more apparently "maker" than others, as scholars like JooYoung Seo and Gabriela Richard (2018) and Katherine Steele, Maya Cakmak, and Brianna Blaser (2018) have argued. Furthermore, the marking of gender difference in the absence of women from this particular space during much of my fieldwork was an experience of disequilibrium for me as I initially struggled to fit in, despite being welcomed. As scholars like Sarah Fox, Rachel Rose Ulgado, and Daniela K. Rosner (2015) and Debbie Chachra (2017) have pointed out, women's disidentification with mainstream (and often male-dominated) makerspaces can be traced to underlying definitions of making that disprivilege practices traditionally associated with women. In other words, the forces of disequilibrium in definitions of "making" and "maker" are as much at play in a makerspace as the forces of disequilibrium in machine malfunctions, user errors, and "failing fast" approaches to prototyping. Therefore, the stories of this chapter focus on the many forces and dimensions of disequilibrium in relations among humans and machines (particularly two of the most prominent fabrication technologies in SoDo Makerspace, the laser cutter and the 3D printers) over several years.

Ready, Fire, Aim

When Eric was bringing me up to speed on the history of SoDo Makerspace in March 2015, he told me that he had acquired the laser cutter six months earlier, in September 2014. He had committed to a paid job on the machine before he and his colleagues were even sure they could operate it. "Right after we got [the laser cutter], we got our first customer call," he recalled as he looked at a photo of the laser cutter in Google Photos on his smartphone (the application organizes photos by date and location, and he was using it to prompt his memory as he recounted the history of SoDo Makerspace). The order was for an etched wooden poster for Seattle's Decibel Festival (an electronic music festival), and it was designed by a local graphic design firm, Soup Standard. Eric realized that "graphic designers needed to know about this place [SoDo Makerspace], because we can take their designs and turn them into objects," and so "we hadn't hooked up the machine, but we'd already committed to the job. Like 'ready, fire, aim.' I knew that if we couldn't get it done here, we could pay to get it done elsewhere; we just needed to start our network," he explained, then swiped to the next picture of the smiling graphic designers holding the finished poster. "Here's the happy recipients," he said. "That was a proud moment." Indeed, much in the way that my telling of this story re-marks the boundaries of how I understand disequilibrium, Eric's account marked (or re-marked) a risky maneuver as a success.

One of the challenges for me, as someone with no prior engineering or hardware training, was learning how software and hardware in SoDo Makerspace communicate and how humans and machines communicate, and I learned that these sites of communication were also frequent sites of disequilibrium—sometimes intentionally, as in the "ready, fire, aim" inaugural job on the laser cutter, and sometimes not, as in the many little laser cutter fires. Some of these sites of disequilibrium are located in the two main communication interfaces associated with the laser cutter: a driver that connects the machine to a desktop computer and software on the desktop computer that connects human users to the machine. Next to the laser cutter is a dedicated computer connected to the machine; this computer has the laser cutter driver—not unlike a desktop inkjet printer driver—that interfaces with the laser cutter, as well as a copy of Inkscape, an open source vector graphics program for designing files (ultimately rendered as tool paths) for the laser cutter. These programs function as interfaces for human-laser cutter communication.

In Inkscape, an image can be rendered into a vector graphic, or a vector graphic can be created from scratch or modified from a template. Different lines can be assigned different colors: for example, blue lines for a border to be cut out, red lines for a design in the middle to be etched. That graphic file can then be exported to the laser cutter driver. In the driver, a person specifies the speed and power for the cut (both expressed as percentages), which are dependent on the material being used and whether the person wants the machine to etch or cut through the material. (Speed and power charts for various materials are made to streamline the trial-and-error process of getting these variables right; in SoDo Makerspace, there were speed and power charts for plywood, leather, and acrylic.) The driver asks for a material thickness measurement, and people usually use a caliper to get a precise measurement, rather than assuming, for example, that plywood sold as 0.25-inch is in fact exactly 0.25 inches thick. The human user also measures and adjusts the machine bed height for the optimum distance between the laser head and the material. The human user also specifies instructions for the various line colors in the file. The vectors, speed and power variables, and material thickness are translated into G code (a series of XYZ coordinates) for the machine's movements. The driver also prompts the person to send the machine through a homing sequence to locate the starting point for the cutting head (which is not itself the laser beam source, but rather a mirror and focusing device for the laser beam, which is located off the back corner of the cutting bed). A small red laser point indicates where the cutting laser beam will be. Experienced users sometimes skip this step and manually step the head on an XY axis (left and right, forward and back) to the starting point.

This file transformation is a key part of the process not only of making things but also of troubleshooting and maintaining machines, and it is not a one-way form of communication. In addition to the necessity of troubleshooting the speed and power specifications, human users also face the necessity of negotiating with the machine's priorities and memory if they try to make changes mid-job. For example, when I observed a start-to-finish project on the laser cutter in April 2015, I watched Eric engage in a series of negotiations with laser cutter, mediated by the driver program. He had a ready-to-go file—a scaled down finger-joint planter box to be cut on plywood—on a USB flash drive that he loaded onto the laser cutter computer, but he couldn't get the program to resize the scale of the object the way he wanted, so he pulled out his smartphone, where he had recorded the original down-scaling calculations, and manually input the measurements in the driver. After turning on the machine's chiller air and exhaust fan system, he instructed the machine to cut on the blue lines in the file at 85% strength (he explained that 70% hadn't been enough to cut through the material last time he'd tried). He turned up the exhaust fan, explaining that it needed to be on a higher setting because cutting through a material generates more smoke and dust, and then he asked the driver for an estimate of how much time it would take the machine to complete the job.

When the laser cutter started cutting, Eric watched the machine cut out the first piece, hoping to see visual evidence that the piece was completely severed from the material—indicated by a slight drop of the cut piece. No such drop occurred, and Eric decided he wanted to slow down the machine (decreasing the speed percentage) to see if that would help the machine cut completely through the material. But when he changed the speed variable in the driver, nothing happened: the machine kept cutting at its original speed. When he realized this, Eric explained to me that the machine was not responsive because it already had memory (for the original job instructions) built up. He shrugged and left the machine to finish its work.

After the machine finished and the laser shut off, Eric opened the glass door and examined the results. The machine had not cut completely through the material, and Eric speculated that perhaps the machine hadn't cut through because the plywood was warped. He had used 3D-printed clamps to flatten the material, but perhaps it hadn't been enough. Or perhaps the lens that focuses the laser was dirty. He decided to send the machine through another cutting sequence to see if the pieces would drop free this time. As the laser cutter worked, he mused, "I'll take a look at the mirrors," and prepared a cotton swab dipped in rubbing alcohol as the machine finished. When the laser cutter completed this job, he inspected the pieces again. The pieces still hadn't been cleanly cut out, but Eric was satisfied: "I'm calling this a success. Most of the pieces can be pushed out [by hand] now." I was struck, in this interaction, as in many of the interactions I observed and engaged at SoDo Makerspace, by the negotiation of the boundaries of "maker" to include both human and machine. Eric's process involved not simply using a tool—inputting instructions into a machine to carry out a task—but negotiating with the machine's memory and output in ways that ultimately redefined his own objective (or what he considered "success").

I didn't understand this at the time, but Lauren, an industrial engineering student (at the time) and former SoDo Makerspace volunteer, later explained to me that a dirty mirror can indeed unfocus the laser beam—not unlike the way a piece of dust on a person's glasses can change that person's vision, she noted. I first met Lauren in SoDo Makerspace in March 2015, when I happened to visit on a day she was volunteering. (Lauren was among the first group of volunteers recruited by Clarissa San Diego). I only saw Lauren in the makerspace that one time, but I used her member contact information on the SoDo Makerspace Trello board (a web-based project management application) to get in touch with her and arrange a meeting in January 2016. Even though Eric had led me through the process of making on the laser cutter, I still didn't entirely understand the machine, especially when it came to human safety and machine maintenance. As Lauren described her experiences in the makerspace to me, she noted that she had been concerned about machine safety, citing the laser cutter as an example.

But human safety is not the only concern in SoDo Makerspace: protecting the laser cutter—whose parts are expensive to replace—is also an ongoing concern. Indeed, a switch on the side of the laser cutter that controls the machine's exhaust fan proved to be another site of disequilibrium in the early months of operating the machine in the makerspace. That fan pulls air through the open space just below the glass door (the space through which Richard reached to hold down the plywood in the Figure 3 video in Chapter 2, https://doi.org/10.3998/mpub.11724511.cmp5) and vents fumes out into an exhaust pipe. Lauren explained that people were turning down the fan—which is quite loud—in an attempt to avoid drowning out conversations, which also functions as a meeting space and houses other (loud) machines. But the lower fan speed meant that dust and smoke were not being properly vented from the system, leading to the accumulation of dirt on the laser lens and the de-focusing of the laser beam. And especially when a user compensated by increasing the laser power instead of cleaning the lens, the laser beam could ignite the dust, and the resulting fire could then overheat and crack the lens—something that happened at least once during Lauren's time at the makerspace. (Until Eric was introduced to a lower-cost provider by his mentor at MakerLabs in Vancouver, BC, in early 2016, a replacement laser lens cost him more than $200.) "One day things were catching on fire [on the cutting bed], and [the people operating the machine] were like, 'oh, the person who taught the [laser cutter certification] class said that was normal,'" she recalled, "but I said, 'no, that is not normal.'"

By the time I observed Eric's prototyping on the laser cutter in April, at least a temporary working solution to the fan and lens cleaning issues was in place. In fact, in March 2015, when Eric sat down with me and recounted the history of SoDo Makerspace, he told me that the month before, "we had a problem with the laser cutter, and I wanted to figure out how to never have it again. It got clogged up and had to be completely deconstructed to find the piece with the clog. So I created a solution with a small fan connected to an LED. If that part ever gets clogged again, the lack of air flow through the fan will cause the light to flash red, and this helps us avoid the expenses of replacing parts." He showed me a video on his smartphone of the process of testing this fan/light solution that allows the laser cutter to indicate to its human users if there is an exhaust/venting problem.

I came to understand that the "ready, fire, aim" interactions Eric and his colleagues had with the laser cutter, particularly in those early months, were entangled with the amateur ethos of SoDo Makerspace, particularly, and of the maker movement. Because I was so utterly unfamiliar with any of the technologies in the space when I began my fieldwork, I tended to view Eric and his colleagues as experts on the laser cutter and other machines (and they certainly were, relative to me). But as I got to know the people and machines, I realized that, particularly in the early months, everyone was an amateur. By contrast, this was very clear to Lauren from the beginning of her involvement with SoDo Makerspace. As an industrial engineering student, she was being trained in the disciplinary-centric model of expertise that the maker movement in many ways resists. After all, the philosophy of a makerspace is to create more access to machines—like laser cutters—that might otherwise only be available to engineers and fabrication specialists. Related to this democratizing impulse is a "learn-by-doing" ethos that encourages hands-on experimentation and troubleshooting. Expertise is not necessarily located in a manual or in a degree, but in experience, which includes and at times vaunts failures. Being self-taught—like many of the regulars in SoDo Makerspace—is a badge of honor in a movement that privileges DIY and encourages people who might not otherwise feel authorized to learn and intervene in processes of design and production that are typically in inaccessible labs and factories.

But in SoDo Makerspace, at least, the "ready, fire, aim" ethos also affected safety and maintenance documentation practices in ways that created (further) disequilibrium, even as they were also inventive and intentional. As I talked to Lauren, I realized that in almost a year of observing people working on the laser cutter, including being led through the process of operating it myself, I'd never seen a set of written instructions (other than a list of prohibited materials, printed from another makerspace's website, laminated, and hung from a lanyard attached to the laser cutter). Indeed, given my own orientation to technical communication, when I first entered the space, I assumed that maker literacies involved writing and reading detailed safety, operation, and maintenance instructions, though certainly, as James Paradis (1991) has observed, even when such manuals exist and are used, they can reduce machines and users to simplified ideals and, in some cases, fail to prevent injury. It seemed that in the early months of laser cutter certifications, the training was conducted primarily through verbal explanation and physical demonstrations of steps and safety protocols, through close observation, and through supervised hands-on experience.

When Lauren was describing her concerns about machine safety in the makerspace—and particularly about information provided to volunteers—she directed me to the SoDo Makerspace wiki, a now-defunct site created by another volunteer who started when she did and who was also concerned about documenting machine safety information, as well as organizing volunteers and co-founders (much in the same way that Eric and Richard, particularly, worked to get other "regulars" to use Trello consistently a year later). The brief entry on the laser cutter was a checklist that includes making sure the "lens [is] clean" and the "air [is] running." By the end of 2015, the wiki site was no longer used or updated, since Lauren and the group of volunteers who started around the same time she did had mostly stopped going to the makerspace. The laser cutter entry, for example, was last updated in December 2014 and as of January 2016 had been accessed 4 times, one of which was by me, and the wiki site has since been deactivated.

Understanding this history of safety protocols led me to realize that the way laser cutter safety and operation information is communicated and practiced is a marking of boundaries. So, too, is the accessibility of safety and operation information (the cost of certification training, the location on the internet and in SoDo Makerspace of written instructions). These boundary markings have consequential implications for who makes (as well as who does not make), how they make, and what they make. As I watched humans and the laser cutter at work, and as I listened to different accounts of engaging with laser cutter safety and operation protocols, I was often reminded of Karen Barad's (2012) concept of "agential cuts," which "do not mark some absolute separation but a cutting together/apart—'holding together' of the disparate itself" (46). Barad's relational theory rejects the notion that knowing is exterior to or separable from being and, therefore, that subjects and objects exist as *a priori* configurations. Instead, knowledges, bodies, and things, are continually made and re-made in what Barad (2007) describes as intra-actions, or "relations without preexisting relata" (139). Subjects and objects are cut together/apart in intra-action: they come to be marked as subject and object in relation. So, too, are humans, machines, and things cut together/apart in intra-actions.

SoDo Makerspace regular Richard Albritton's intra-action with the laser cutter re-marked human-machine boundaries (Figure 3, https://doi .org/10.3998/mpub.11724511.cmp5) as Richard's proprioception encompassed both his own fingers and the movements of the laser beam passing near his fingers as they pressed a warped piece of plywood flat to ensure the speed and power settings would work as calculated—even though this practice was discouraged in shop rules and machine operation manuals. But in Lauren's case, her desire for more safety protocols was at odds with the prevalent practices in SoDo Makerspace, leading to a re-marking of boundaries as she ultimately decided to remove herself from those practices. The boundary (re)marking in Lauren's departure led to another boundary (re)marking: with her departure (as with the departure of other women who had been involved in the early months of makerspace operations), the gender balance in SoDo Makerspace skewed further male-identified. This boundary (re)marking in turn shaped my own experience in the space, and it inevitably shaped what got made (and what didn't), for whom, and by whom. After all, as feminist scholars like Donna Haraway (1991) have long argued, design is not an objective act but a "view from somewhere" (196), and the positionality of that view matters for what gets made, and for whom.

The negotiation of strength-and-power settings on the laser cutter— much like the negotiation of the boundaries of makers and practices across SoDo Makerspace—was ongoing. I heard Eric address the issue of documentation when he was experimenting with etching fabric dye into pieces of acrylic on the laser cutter in July 2015. As I describe in Chapter Three, during that summer, SoDo Makerspace participated in the Seattle Youth Employment Program (SYEP), in which institutionally identified "at-risk" youth were paid by the city and placed in participating local businesses as volunteers/apprentices. A group from SYEP was in the makerspace helping with an art project for the community wall, and a Seattle police officer from the department's community outreach section was there visiting with the SYEP participants and chatting with Eric as he experimented. (The officer told me his outreach to the youth included inviting them on all-day ride-alongs.) As they chatted, the fabric dye ignited, starting a small fire on the cutting bed, and Eric quickly switched off the machine. No harm was done, but once Eric had recovered the piece of acrylic, the officer asked, "So are you writing down what you're trying [on the machine]?" to which Eric replied, "In an ideal situation, we'd be writing down everything we try, but I'm just doing it on the fly." And when he realized that the machine hadn't burned the color from the fabric dye into the etched marks (an outline of the Seattle skyline) on the clear acrylic, he dabbed his fingers in the dyes (blue and green, for the Seattle Seahawks) and rubbed the colors into the etching until they showed up. "I'm calling this a success," he said.

But not all disequilibrium is tolerated or framed as an opportunity for success. (And, indeed, just as I observed in the previous chapter that the identity of "maker" is felt and negotiated differently for different bodies and different situations, so too is "success" differentially felt and negotiated.) Seven months later, in January 2016 (not long after my conversation with Lauren), an incident with the laser cutter resulted in written documentation regarding laser cutter maintenance in the form of a blog post on the SoDo Makerspace site, as well as changes to the laser cutter's exhaust system. Tony Loiseleur, who was at the time a self-described "shop assistant" and lead blog writer at SoDo Makerspace (as we saw in the previous chapter), described this incident in a January 26, 2016, blog post on the SoDo Makerspace website titled "Making and the Art of Laser Maintenance." After several hours of cutting stencils for a start-up incubated at the makerspace, the fairly new lens cracked, but "as best as we can figure, the reason [it] broke wasn't because we had been using [it] for hours on end—apparently, the manufacturer claims that it's able to run for eight hours straight, no problem—but rather a number of minor maintenance problems coming together to make for a perfect storm of lens destruction," Tony explained in the post.

Eric and a colleague who has an undergraduate engineering degree went through the now-familiar steps of cleaning with rubbing alcohol and cotton swabs and checking the exhaust system. Despite Eric's efforts in creating the LED light solution to alert human users to a fan problem, the exhaust system had "unfortunately gone without much maintenance" over the last several months, according to Tony, so Eric and his colleague took apart and cleaned the fan. They also adjusted the bearings on the fan, which showed signs of heat damage, and they added a second fan and installed additional ducting for both fans. The implementation of the exhaust system upgrades was not only an effort to prevent future lens cracks but also an anticipation of an upgrade in the laser bulb. The laser had operated with a 90-watt bulb until January, and Eric had arranged to purchase a 130-watt bulb as part of a bulk order placed by his mentor at MakerLabs in Vancouver (in fact, he called this "a first step" in the regional makerspace network he hoped to establish). The new bulb was installed in late January, and because it is more powerful than its predecessor, laser cutter users had to recalibrate strength-and-power settings for various materials.

In February 2016, I observed Eric troubleshooting with these settings on a ¾-inch piece of wood flooring (which the previous bulb would not have cut through). The previous week, while we were eating lunch at a nearby bakery, Eric had told me that as a result of his experiences in SoDo Makerspace, he had figured out how to solve a problem in his house that he wouldn't have known how to solve before: an uneven spot in his wood flooring that needed a custom-sized replacement piece. "I realized that I could take a pencil and a piece of paper and push the paper down into the spot and trace it in 3D, and then just cut a matching piece [of flooring] to fit," he explained. "And then I started thinking it would be cool to cut out designs in a piece of flooring for my kids' rooms—like their names, or shapes."

Indeed, disequilibrium is a reality in SoDo Makerspace, whether it is being cultivated in rapid prototyping practices or it is an unintended by-product of operations in what Eric calls a "bootstrapped" makerspace. I can attest that continual exposure to disequilibrium (and the resulting problem-solving processes), even from a researcher's perspective, affected how I thought about problems and invention—from fixing things around the house to prototyping this book—in a way similar to what Eric described in his DIY flooring solution. The following week, as I watched, Eric experimented with cutting out puzzle piece shapes in a piece of wood flooring. This time, he was noting the strength-and-power settings directly on the piece of wood, next to various cuts (Figure 6).

While Eric was not recording these settings in the way that I suspect the police officer meant (months earlier) when he asked Eric if he was writing down what he was trying, these notes were certainly guiding Eric's efforts in this particular project. In this case, the product and the documentation were one and the same, which was useful for Eric, but not necessarily useful for distributing to other machine users. Just as James Paradis (1991) notes that the "operator's manual becomes a kind of script for the human-machine interface, in which human physiology is unified with machine action" (13), Eric's markings on the cuts became both a script and an interface for human-machine interaction.

Figure 6. Eric documents speed and power settings on project material

Eric had, the day before, found a strength-and-power combination that successfully cut through the practice piece, and he was now attempting to recreate that cut on a new piece. But the settings that had worked before were not working this time, and the puzzle pieces were not dropping free. Eric offered several reasons for this: the flooring piece could have a slight difference in thickness from the practice piece, or this piece (or the practice piece) could be slighted warped, or there might be a different amount of moisture in the air or in the material, or there could have been a temperature difference. "Too many variables to track and write down," he added. "It's easier to just get through it." (Indeed, this was not an unusual philosophy of documentation in SoDo Makerspace.)

And this brings us to the little laser cutter fire that begins this chapter. Eric instructed the laser cutter (via the driver) to make another pass, this time at a slower speed, and after it began cutting, he turned away to set his practice piece (with the notes) on a nearby table. Out of the corner of my eye, I saw a flame on the laser cutter bed through the glass door, and I called Eric back. He grabbed his water bottle and opened the machine door, which automatically shut off the laser. The fire went out with the rush of air (Figure 7), and Eric removed the burned pieces. (Now that I've seen fires on the laser cutter, Eric's "ready, fire, aim" metaphor at the beginning of this chapter has taken on a whole new meaning.) He speculated that the fire might have been caused by having the laser make another pass when the material was still hot from the previous pass, or perhaps the speed setting was too slow. He made a note on the burned pieces of the speed and power settings on the pass when the fire occurred (Figure 7). Eric then removed the cutting bed and opened a panel on the front of the machine, pulling out a tray full of bits of materials from previous cuts. He dumped the tray in the trash and grabbed a broom to reach further back into the machine to try to sweep out still more pieces. "It's only gonna be as nice to me as I am to it," he pointed out as he cleaned. One of Eric's colleagues walked in and saw Eric crouched in front of the laser cutter with a broom. "Just a little fire in the laser cutter," I said, and he nodded.

Two weeks later, in mid-February, I saw a printed set of daily, weekly, and monthly maintenance steps for the laser cutter sitting on the laser computer station, and I learned that Eric's colleague with an engineering degree had produced them. When I saw the instructions, I was reminded of the now-defunct wiki instructions Lauren had shown me. There are similarities: both sets of instructions offer a checklist and attend to the fan/exhaust system, but while the wiki instructions seem to focus on daily use, the engineer's instructions include many more steps and include longer-term maintenance. While, as both Lauren and Eric had told me, the regular users of SoDo Makerspace in its early months were mostly "amateurs" (their word), the addition of two "experts" (a word used by Eric and Tony to describe both the engineer and Alex, the 3D-printing guru) in late 2015 seemed to have tempered the "ready, fire, aim" ethos and brought about changes in the troubleshooting and documentation practices with the laser cutter and 3D printers.

I asked Tony if he'd worked on this set of laser cutter instructions, since I knew he was invested in making more written documentation for training and machine maintenance and had helped with written instructions for the 3D printer certification. "Yeah, no. I wish I could have edited them, though," Tony replied. "Did you see how it says 'monthy,' like without the *l*?" (In fact, someone had handwritten an *l* in the misspelled word.) "Stuff like that could make us look bad, like we're not accurate," he continued. Just as the engineer had provided a correction to problems in the exhaust system and problems with human maintenance of the laser cutter, Tony

Figure 7. A little fire in the laser cutter

saw his expertise in writing and copyediting as providing a correction to the professional image of the space, particularly in its written artifacts.

Embodied Knowing

As I considered the contrast in these laser cutter instructions (which, I should note, were no longer displayed by 2018, by which point the engineer had moved on to a new venture, and were eventually replaced by more extensive operating instructions) and a "ready, fire, aim" approach, I pondered Eric's remark that it was easier to "just get through it." This reminded me of what he'd said to the police officer seven months earlier—that "in an ideal situation" notes would be recorded on strength-and-power combinations. I was struck by the realization that, in this situation, learning by doing was perhaps a more effective, or at least realistic, way of documenting than attempting to record everything in writing. I came to understand Eric's "learning by doing" as an embodied, distributed practice involving written notes to himself, numerical instructions to the laser cutter via the driver, remembered experiences, machine memory, materials, the climate of the place, and experimentation with settings. Like Alex's 3D printing instructions that included print samples (Figure 5, Chapter 3, https://doi.org/10.3998/mpub.11724511.cmp8), Eric's documentation of speed and power charts and laser cutter settings were almost always done on the material in question, reminding me that in such a 3D-oriented space, incorporating 3D objects into technical writing can be an effective and necessary approach to complement embodied knowing in a makerspace.

Another important factor in practice of embodied knowing, I've learned, is time. Alex measured Tony's training on 3D printers in spools of filament. Over time (or, specifically, "after you've used up a spool or two"), Alex told Tony, "You'll get a feel for things," including learning how to "eyeball" things that initially require machine- or tool-aided measurement. In fact, "getting a feel for things" often results in a kind of cyborg embodiment wherein a human's sensibilities—including proprioception, like eyeballing 3D printer measurements or knowing a (relatively) safe distance between fingers and laser beam—extend to include the appendages and movements of a machine. (Or, in a less human-centric sense, a human body is recalibrated to a machine.)

But sometimes this embodied cyborg knowing goes awry, resulting in disequilibrium. This disequilibrium is a kind of making, including the making of literal marks on bodies, both human and machine. I witnessed a few small nicks and cuts on human bodies (usually hands) in SoDo Makerspace, and Clarissa told me that there was a more serious finger injury on the CNC mill in the early months of SoDo Makerspace. I also observed that the laser cutter fire I described above (Figure 7) left a permanent light-gray burn mark on the laser cutter's grated cutting bed, and in the aforementioned blog post, "Making and the Art of Laser Maintenance," Tony documented burn marks on the bearings of the laser cutter's fan engine as a result of a lack of regular maintenance and readjustments.

In fact, embodied knowing or learning often happens *through* disequilibrium, including the making of mistakes and physical marks, which are often themselves embodied things that take on a life of their own or change future makings. For example, "failed" 3D prints often take on a life of their own that exceeds or diverges from the original purpose. Richard noticed when he was 3D printing a skull (for Halloween) on one of the MakerBots that the filament was unusually stringy because it had absorbed moisture from the air (and in the fall in the Pacific Northwest, there is considerable moisture in the air), creating a webbed effect where there should have been open spaces. Months later, I learned in a conversation with Alex that this is called filament "snot" and that "snotty" prints can be avoided by storing filament in airtight containers. Alex implemented this practice with the filament for his 3D printers, though the filament spools for the MakerBots, which Richard continued to use, were still stored in the open air above the machines. Still, while "snot" is generally undesirable in 3D prints, the effect was fitting for a Halloween skull, which was on display in the maker-space for months on a shelf of 3D-printed curiosities.

And I'd only known Alex for a few weeks when he offered me a "failed print" of a small vase printed from PET filament (the same material soda bottles are made from) that looked surprisingly like etched glass. Alex kept all his "failed" prints in a clear plastic box (just below his 3D print-ers) labeled "FAILED (But Still Cool) PRINTS." Much like the assortment of 3D-printed objects displayed on a nearby shelf, these objects not only helped people adjust settings for future prints but also serve to illustrate techniques and possibilities to others, like people taking the 3D printer certification class.

Mistakes or other problems—like warped materials, design flaws, or malfunctioning machine parts—can also result in unexpected entangle-ments of human and machine labor, as was the case when Richard used his fingers to flatten warped plywood on the laser cutter (Figure 3, https://doi .org/10.3998/mpub.11724511.cmp5). And that day in April 2015 when I observed Eric prototyping and troubleshooting on the laser cutter, he was simultaneously engaged in trying to fix a filament jam in the extruder piece of one of the MakerBots, which, at the time, were the primary 3D printers in SoDo Makerspace. He ended up having to stand next to the machine with his arm in the top of the machine, applying pressure to the extruder with his hand, or as he put it, literally "giving the machine a hand."

Similarly, when Clarissa San Diego described to me (via Skype in 2016) her experience of learning to use the CNC machine, which she referred to as one of her favorite machines, along with the laser cutter, she mentioned not only time and her own mistakes but also problems with the machine itself as integral to her learning process. Like Eric's first job on the laser cutter, making a poster for a graphic design firm, Clarissa's first job on the CNC was a "ready, fire, aim" job for a client who had commissioned six-foot-tall marquis-light letters made from lavender foam. "I loved it because it was a huge learning process for me," she recalled. "I made tons of mis-takes; I failed; I wasted material, money, and time. But after it was done, I really felt that satisfaction of, 'Wow, I made this,' and the next time going around was way easier."

And it wasn't just that Clarissa experienced a learning curve on that particular process: "At the time, our CNC machine was acting up every other hour, and that's when I got really intimate with the CNC. I was like, 'All right, [laughs] I'm gonna get to know you in and out because you keep breaking on me and I need to know how to fix you.'" She paused, and continued, "And that's kind of been the case: it's just always not being afraid to fail, understanding that when things go wrong, there's a process to figure out how to make it right. And it's so great—once we turned on all the marquis lights, you just kind of forgot all that, it was just, 'Wow, it was worth it.'" Indeed, Clarissa modeled giving time and being willing to allow for mistakes and understandings both in relationships with machines and in relationships with other people.

Furthermore, in following decolonial scholars' call to acknowledge epistemological foundations (Haas 2012) and to de-exceptionalize theoretical traditions (Cortez 2017), I set these observations and experiences of embodied knowing in a makerspace alongside Indigenous rhetorical traditions that emphasize practices of embodied knowing and did so long before the contemporary maker movement. Gabriela Raquel Ríos (2015) explains that "land-based rhetorics recognize the ways in which nature can *produce* relations," and, in turn, land-based literacies describe "a relationship between land and bodies that produces knowledge, and that knowledge provides a 'context in which process, product, and self might become one'" (65, quoting Cajete). Kristen Arola (2018) describes an Indigenous ethic of making that involves "putting yourself into the objects you bring into the world so as to honor the relations that came before and will come after" (275–276). While I had initially understood embodied knowledge in a (Western humanist) way that focuses on an individual human body at an individual moment in time, Ríos's and Arola's articulations of embodied and embodying knowledge remind me that humans and environments are in co-constituting relations that extend beyond the present. These scholars remind us that the distributed processes of extending human memory, like the ones I observed in the context of the contemporary maker movement, are also not exceptional or original to the maker movement or to Western technological traditions. These scholars model a more than humanist way of understanding and practicing making that is accountable to relations and marks on bodies past, present, and future.

Who Makes?

Clarissa's referring to the CNC in second person, as someone she got to know well, is an example of a tendency among many of the people in my study to anthropomorphize machines. This anthropomorphizing is another practice of disequilibrium that reconfigures the boundaries of human and nonhuman. Consider, for example, Eric's "giving the [MakerBot] a hand" and his observation that the laser cutter would only "be as nice to me as I am to it," as well as Alex's practice of giving the machines he builds names (like Little Millie and Big Buddha) that are different from the official product names he eventually gives them. Anthropomorphizing is a form of disequilibrium that disrupts a human-focused system (in this case, who counts as a maker) by reconfiguring boundaries. Sociologist and science and technology studies scholar Janet Vertesi (2015) describes a similar phenomenon as "agential gerrymandering," or "linguistically drawing and redrawing the boundaries between human and machine," in her account of the use of the pronoun "we" in reference to Mars rovers by scientists and engineers on the Rover missions (189).

Beyond anthropomorphizing and agential gerrymandering in how people talk about machines, learning to interact with the machines as co-makers is part of the embodied process of becoming a maker. In addition to the expansion of proprioception to include both machine and human appendages, there is also an expansion of who and what count as a maker. We might even call it "significant prosthesis," to borrow Donna Haraway's term. As Haraway (1988) explains, "Embodiment is significant prosthesis: objectivity cannot be about fixed vision when what counts as an object is precisely what world history turns out to be about" (588). Or as Karen Barad (2007) puts it, "Bodies in the making are never separate from their apparatuses of bodily production" (159).

Mattering as a maker—becoming a body recognized as a maker—is not solely the purview of humans, but neither are all humans made to matter as makers. In some ways, the laser cutter, the 3D printers, and the CNC machines are addressed as "makers" more than some people: particularly those who do not engage in the kinds of making practiced in SoDo Makerspace and the maker movement—a reminder that the maker movement and the technologies associated with it are not neutral. While other forms of disequilibrium in SoDo Makerspace can be sites of invention and possibility, this disequilibrium, or boundary markings that create imbalances in who and what count as makers, is a site of exclusion and foreclosure. While the makerspace regulars are committed to increasing diversity in the space and access to fabrication technologies, critics of the maker movement and tech industries, including Debbie Chachra (2017) and Amy Nguyen (2015), have pointed out that the privileging of the kinds of making associated with the maker movement and the tech industry is a privileging of traditionally male practices. Indeed, the definition of "maker" in SoDo Makerspace and the maker movement does seem to be tied to certain kinds of making (often involving heavy, expensive machinery) and not other kinds of making, like the kinds of making that often get labeled "crafting" and that are traditionally associated with women and Indigenous peoples.

There are also definitions of making that are set by the design of technologies and spaces themselves and the bodies those designs privilege. Indeed, Katherine Steele, Maya Cakmak, and Brianna Blaser (2018) describe touring another makerspace in Seattle (on the University of Washington campus, just a few miles north of SoDo Makerspace) with a group of students with diverse abilities and observing the complexities of how the design of the space mattered differently to different bodies:

> For example, one student noted, "I really like that almost everything is on wheels, because as a person in a wheelchair it's a lot easier to get something out of your way." Furniture on wheels made it easier for her to navigate the space and customize the space to her needs. However, a student with a visual impairment voiced that she found the wheeled furniture a bit concerning: "With a visual impairment, I create mental maps to navigate spaces. I love that all of the furniture is on wheels to create flexibility, but I also liked that a lot of the tools are in fixed spots. I will always know the location of the 3-D printer and laser cutter, even if the space in between changes from day to day." (116)

Indeed, as Karen Barad (2007) argues in her feminist and ethics-focused concept of agential realism, "Accountability to marks on bodies requires an accounting of the apparatuses that enact determinate causal structures, boundaries, properties, and meanings" (341). In a makerspace, those apparatuses include human-machine intra-actions, safety and operations protocols and practices, and the kinds of bodies (gendered, dis/abled, raced, classed, etc.) that are more readily marked as "makers."

Indeed, relative privilege matters in how people experience disequilibrium. As I described earlier, Lauren, the industrial engineering student and former SoDo Makerspace volunteer, had an abundance of maker skills and literacies (including experience and training in fabrication) recognized by her colleagues in SoDo Makerspace, but her views on documentation, as well as the organization and recognition of volunteer labor, differed with the practices of SoDo Makerspace leadership. In this case, boundary marks between Lauren's identifications and expectations and those of the leadership led to her departure, which reconfigured gender relations in the space (so much so that I was often the only woman in the space for much of my fieldwork after Lauren's departure). That departure also reconfigured the boundaries and relations of this study, as my conversation with Lauren enriched and nuanced my understanding of what I was observing and experiencing in SoDo Makerspace. Lauren, in turn, connected me with Clarissa San Diego, and that relationship reconfigured boundaries of understandings and engagements in and beyond this study, as I explain in Chapter 3 and in the next chapter.

And just as documentation practices and fabrication technologies can themselves be barriers to a human's being recognized as a maker (because they may be intimidating, or because they might not correspond with what that human wants to make), not all nonhuman makers are granted equal status by their human users. Consider, for example, the MakerBot 3D printers that were the primary 3D printers in SoDo Makerspace in its first two years. Eric and Richard (in particular) frequently expressed their annoyance with the MakerBots—and usually in the same breath—the company that makes them. For example, when Eric was giving the MakerBot's jammed extruder a hand, he remarked that the extruder was a "piece of shit" and said, "I can't believe [MakerBot] puts their name on it."

He added that the replacement part was sold out—probably because they all break so quickly, he speculated—and that he would have to pay $100 to talk to customer service or buy another entire MakerBot printer, neither of which he was willing to do. Instead, he said, he had taken apart an extruder from the malfunctioning printer's predecessor model and was determined to learn how to fix it himself. Though MakerBot was closely aligned with the maker movement, Eric was not alone in his irritation with its 3D printers (and the extruders, specifically). As Richard explained to me in fall 2015, MakerBot fell out of favor with some makers not only because of alleged issues with quality and customer service but also because the company's response to increased competition in the 3D printer market was to make what had once been open-source hardware and software closed source, a decision Richard called "shortsighted."

In February 2016, Alex, Tony, and Richard were discussing a set of panic buttons (each played a different sound when pressed) that Eric had bought to put at each machine, and Richard joked that the one that played a trumpet fanfare sound should be assigned to the MakerBots to be played "if they ever execute a flawless print—so basically never." (By 2017, the MakerBots were no longer in use or displayed in SoDo Makerspace and had been replaced by open-source 3D printers.) In fact, I noticed that at the beginning, Richard was the only cofounder who already knew how to operate all the machines in the makerspace (because of his prior experience at another Seattle makerspace that closed just before SoDo Makerspace opened) and thus was often responsible for helping with problem-solving and training people on all the machines. But over time, the arrival of other experts—like the engineer who was "the laser guy" (Tony's words), and Alex, "the 3D printer genius" (Eric's words)—allowed Richard to focus more on his own interest and expertise in small electronics. Indeed, Tony referred to Richard as "our electronics maven" in a February 18, 2016, blog post on the SoDo Makerspace website entitled "LEDiva Revision B Testing." While this disequilibrium at the level of the SoDo Makerspace system—the shift away from the amateur ethos that characterized the early months—opened up new possibilities for making for Richard, the increased emphasis on fabrication expertise also made it more difficult for Tony to make space for himself and have his ethos recognized in the makerspace.

The disequilibrium between the maker-movement-inspired amateur/ DIY ethos and the increased privileging of fabrication expertise parallels an economic disequilibrium in the production and revenue systems of SoDo Makerspace that, in turn, parallels other descriptions of makerspaces. Indeed, Silvia Lindtner and David Li (2012) have observed that "financial sustainability is a constant issue for hackerspaces and the subject of continuous reflection" (n.p.), and I found this to be true in SoDo Makerspace. SoDo Makerspace, like the maker movement, framed itself as a rapid prototyping space for inventors, entrepreneurs, artists, hobbyist, small business owners, kids, and others who might not otherwise have access to such technologies. The reality, though, is that rapid prototyping activities—sometimes a one-off weekend project for a hobbyist, or an occasional prototype for an inventor—are not necessarily a steady or significant revenue generator.

Clarissa designed the à la carte pricing model that SoDo Makerspace initially relied on to be responsive to the fact that many clients of makerspaces are hobbyists who would rather pay as they go for certifications and machine time than buy a monthly membership to the space. Indeed, SoDo Makerspace rose out of the ashes of another makerspace that operated on a membership model. SoDo Makerspace also sought other sources of income, including fulfilling production orders for clients and incubating products for mass distribution and taking a percentage of the profits. In its last year of operations, SoDo Makerspace transitioned to a membership model. While SoDo Makerspace maintained what Eric described as a solid membership base through 2018, rising rents in Seattle made it difficult for membership revenue to offset the costs of operating, which contributed to Eric's decision to close SoDo Makerspace when the lease for the space ended in October 2018.

Like other makerspaces and the maker movement more broadly, SoDo Makerspace positioned itself as disruptive, in the sense of democratizing access to prototyping technologies. But SoDo Makerspace was also reliant on traditional, globalized, capitalist systems of production. For example, a product prototyped in SoDo Makerspace was ultimately mass produced from parts produced in other countries that were assembled in and distributed from an international production and distribution facility near the makerspace. SoDo Makerspace did indeed democratize access to prototyping technologies and thus create opportunities (at least for some bodies), but it did so within, not outside of, global, capitalist forces of disequilibrium.

Furthermore, SoDo Makerspace was also susceptible to the forces of capitalism, particularly in its continual negotiations of revenue and profit-sharing models and ultimately in the CEO's decision to close the space in 2018. In an interesting coincidence, Techshop, an international chain of makerspaces upon which many local makerspaces (like SoDo Makerspace) were modeled, closed all its US locations in November 2017, about a year before SoDo Makerspace closed. In an editorial note introducing TechShop's CEO Dan Woods's announcement, on November 15, 2017, of the closure of US locations and plans to file for bankruptcy, the editors of *Make: Magazine* wrote,

> We've been following the life, good times and troubles, of TechShop for several years. Many members of the community looked toward TechShop as a possible model of running a makerspace as a business. At this point, it is safe to say that this experiment is over. Hopefully we can look back and break down what worked, and what didn't so that we can do what makers do best: learn from the past. (n.p.)

And as maker communities around the United States reflected on the closure of TechShop in 2017, Clarissa San Diego's growing Makerologist agency (formed with several other alumni of SoDo Makerspace) was positioning itself as an agency and *not* a makerspace.

Two years later, in June 2019, Maker Media, an investor-funded company led by Dale Dougherty that published *Make: Magazine* and managed maker faires, shut down and filed for bankruptcy, leaving the future of the magazine and faires in question. One month later, Dougherty announced the formation of Make Community, a member-funded organization, explaining,

> As you may have heard, Maker Media Inc. went out of business in June 2019. Although I sincerely appreciate the investors who helped us grow, we couldn't provide a sufficient return on their investment. I know that our mission to empower makers is valuable and important because I have seen and heard about its impact on people's lives. Because of this, I couldn't bear to see Make: and Maker Faire go away, so I have acquired all the assets of Maker Media and placed them in a new organization, Make Community LLC. As I reflect on the last 15 years and think about what we've done and who we are, the most important is how we have helped to organize and grow and shape the community of maker-minded people in our country and around the world. (2019, n.p.)

Dougherty describes Make Community as "a voluntary association—an organization dedicated to serving its members. By joining, you will help protect the value of Make: [Magazine] and Maker Faire and ensure that we can sustain our work for future makers" (2019, n.p.). Like many in and beyond the maker movement, I am curious to observe how the future of Make Community unfolds, and the extent to which it remains central to the global maker movement.

These disequilibria in the local makerspace and in the global maker movement led to a productive disequilibrium in the scope of my study and of this book. This project began as a study of (and book about) a makerspace and then became about people whose paths intersected that makerspace as I realized how dynamic the configurations of people in the makerspace were. But as SoDo Makerspace closed (and TechShop and Maker Media filed for bankruptcy), and new configurations of makers and spaces emerged, I realized that this study and this book needed to look beyond the walls of a single space, and also beyond the model of the makerspace. Furthermore, as I observed local and global disequilibria in the maker movement, I was becoming increasingly wary of importing the language and practices of the maker movement into my classrooms without also critically engaging disequilibria in the maker movement—from issues of equity and inclusion to issues of sustainability. Thus, while I am still compelled by the possibilities of disequilibrium in and beyond the classroom, I also proceed with attention to the boundaries marked by rhetorical forces of disequilibrium. To account for definitions and practices of making beyond a makerspace, and to articulate the community-focused approach that guides my application of maker-inspired pedagogies (including disequilibrium), I turn in the next chapter to Clarissa San Diego's philosophy and practice of making community.

CHAPTER FIVE

Community

"If you design the right kind of community, that community can make anything." Clarissa San Diego, founder and CEO of Makerologist, offered this insight in March 2019, as we were catching up on one of her latest projects over video conference, which was also the platform for our first conversation-turned-collaboration in 2016. Clarissa's insight about community is core to her philosophy, in and beyond the maker movement, and her philosophy shapes not only her own practice, but also my own practices, including the making of this book. This project began as a study of a makerspace and then became about people whose paths intersected that makerspace as I realized how dynamic the configurations of people in the makerspace were. As a result, while Chapters 3 and 4 focus primarily on acts of making in SoDo Makerspace, this chapter and the following chapter look at acts and implications of making beyond the walls of the makerspace. Furthermore, SoDo Makerspace's closing and Makerologist's emerging (amid the backdrop of the closure and bankruptcy of the influential TechShop chain of makerspaces in the United States, as well as the bankruptcy of Maker Media) led me to realize that this study and this book needed to look not only beyond the walls of a makerspace but also beyond the model of a makerspace. This, I believe, is where the maker movement can learn, as I have, from Clarissa's relational, community-focused philosophy and practice.

I have observed—along with makers and scholars who have said it before me—that definitions of making in the maker movement tend to focus on the fabrication technologies that often anchor makerspaces: 3D printing, laser cutting, CNC milling, soldering, sewing, and more. There is a wide range in the locations of makerspaces (around the world and within a particular city—in schools, in libraries, in industrial neighborhoods, in community centers), in the funding and leadership structures of maker-spaces (grant-funded, co-ops, for-profit, subsidized by a government or educational institution), and in the kinds of people, languages, skills, and projects in makerspaces. But the presence of these fabrication technologies tends to be one of the key "family resemblances" in an otherwise heterog-enous global movement, as Silvia Lindtner, Shaowen Bardzell, and Jeffrey Bardzell (2016) observe (1392). Perhaps not surprisingly, guides for creat-ing a makerspace—like Maker Media's (2013) *Makerspace Playbook*—often begin with a focus on acquiring, learning, maintaining, and teaching others to use fabrication technologies like 3D printers and laser cutters.

Clarissa's community-focused philosophy is a revision of one of the rhetorical topoi (or commonly held understandings) of the maker move-ment: that with the right tools and skills, anyone can make anything. Cla-rissa's formulation—"If you design the right kind of community, any com-munity can make anything"—reminds us that there's more to making than tools and skills and individual people. Her formulation also reminds us that creating and sustaining community is a precondition for meaningful prac-tices of making. And her emphasis on the design of communities reminds us that creating and sustaining community is as much a rhetorical *techne* (or skillful practice) as fabricating 3D objects or designing technologies. I have witnessed Clarissa's philosophy in action in her professional practice as a community strategist and as founder and CEO of Makerologist, which she designed not as a makerspace but as a collective of people who work with maker technologies (broadly defined) and who are connected by re-lationships, skills, projects, clients, and shared commitments to sustaining communities. I have also witnessed Clarissa's philosophy in action in our collaborations, both in Makerologist contexts (for example, cofacilitating team writing activities) and in academic contexts (for example, coauthoring and copresenting papers).

Clarissa has taught me to understand making in a more than human but still human-centered way. In other words, Clarissa has taught me that making is about relationships, and those relationships are not just among humans. Therefore, this chapter offers an account of developing a collab-orative partnership with Clarissa that is inspired by her work as a commu-nity strategist in the maker movement and related industries. The chapter then discusses how Clarissa applies prototyping strategies to the making of communities. Finally, the chapter concludes with a section of advice on making from people in this study, including Clarissa, as well as my own advice for teachers and researchers of making in its many forms.

From Writing About to Writing With

Our collaboration began when I interviewed Clarissa (via Skype) in January 2016, after Lauren, a former SoDo Makerspace volunteer, connected us. Clarissa had moved from Seattle to San Francisco around the time I began my study of the makerspace. I asked Clarissa about diversity and inclusion in the makerspace, since there were relatively few women and people of color who were regulars in the makerspace at the time. At this point, the interview turned into a discussion of issues of diversity and inclusion in the maker movement and in technology industries, since we had both been thinking about and observing these issues from our different perspectives as a researcher and a practitioner, and as a white woman and a woman of color. Clarissa reminded me then, and many times in the following years, that definitions like "diversity" and "inclusion" need to be localized and contextualized, rather than blanket assumptions we start with.

Indeed, Clarissa's contextualized, dynamic approach to negotiating diversity and inclusion resonates with intersectional approaches to identity. For example, Karen Barad (2007) reads Leela Fernandes's (1997) ethnographic study of the intersections of gender and class in Calcutta jute mills as exemplary of the dynamic, nuanced understandings afforded by such an approach:

> In Fernandes' hands, for example, identity formation is understood not in terms of a Euclidean geometrical model but as a dynamics of changing topologies of space, time, and matter. Identity, in her account, is not about location or positionality with respect to a Euclidean grid of identification. Rather, identity formation is a contingent and contested ongoing material process; "identities" are mutually constituted and (re)configured through one another in dynamic intra-relationship with the iterative (re)configuring of relations of power. (240–241)

Clarissa, likewise, negotiates the marking of identity and difference through situated, unfolding relations of power, as the stories in this chapter show.

And in addition to redefining my orientation to difference, that moment with Clarissa on Skype also redefined my understanding of relational knowledge making. In that conversation, we both articulated that we wanted to write about inclusion, and we agreed to collaborate and keep thinking and talking about inclusion and access. Thus, we began to redefine the boundaries between researcher and participant and between academic and practitioner. Our iterative, collaborative analysis revealed to us four key dimensions of community strategy practices that we described in a coauthored article for *Technical Communication*: localizing communities, localizing goals, localizing communication, and localizing inclusion. While we initially identified these dimensions (each of which is a boundary-marking practice) in our interpretation of Clarissa's work as a practitioner, we realized they also applied to our own collaborative knowledge making (Shivers-McNair and San Diego 2017).

Over the course of several months, as we generated, analyzed, and told stories about community strategy, we developed a practice of comaking knowledge that has carried forward in our many and varied collaborations since writing that first article. We told each other stories about experiences and about scholarly and professional frameworks. We recorded our stories, we revisited and reviewed our stories, and we made new stories— and in so doing, we also made new connections and understandings in our relationship and in our practices. While our initial goals were focused on our respective researcher and practitioner communities, our ongoing collaborative work has brought both our goals and communities together. For example, Clarissa connected me with other practitioners in the Seattle area, including the Makerologist team, which led to cofacilitations of team writing and ongoing collaborations with other Makerologist team members. And in addition to being a featured speaker at the Multilingual UX Symposium I helped organize in November 2017 at the University of Texas at El Paso and a copresenter with me at the 2018 Association of Teachers of Technical Writing Conference, Clarissa facilitated discussions and workshops in courses I taught at the University of Washington and the University of Arizona.

Community Strategy in and beyond the Maker Movement

In my ongoing work with Clarissa, I have come to understand that she recognizes every space she enters as "filled with complementing skills sets waiting to achieve bigger goals," words she used to describe the room where she gave a featured talk at the inaugural Multilingual User Experience Symposium at the University of Texas at El Paso in November 2017. This is, in a nutshell, Clarissa's philosophy and practice of community strategy. She combines a commitment to humans—as individuals, as personal connections, as different bodies—with a commitment to more-than-human possibilities for collaboration, innovation, and justice through combinations of humans, human skills, technologies, and other resources.

As we argue in our 2017 *Technical Communication* article, Clarissa's definition and practice of community strategy emphasizes relationship and community building not only between designers and users/stakeholders, but also among users, stakeholders, and communities. Thus, community strategy starts with relationships and leverages those relationships to identify issues and problems and to create localized, sustainable designs. In this way, Clarissa's practice of community strategy bridges (or reconfigures the boundaries of) developer localization, which Huatong Sun (2012) defines as "the localization work occurring at the developer's site that we commonly refer to when thinking of localization," and user localization, which is the "energetic user efforts of using a technology within meaningful social practices and incorporating the technology into one's life" (40). To connect developers and user communities, Clarissa draws on her knowledge and experience in hardware and software—one example is in her producing a tutorial that implemented a past employer's microcontroller along with coding instructions for a simple solution for finding a phone set on silent for Hackster.io, an online community focused on hardware. She also organized the DevRel Summit, a one-day conference featuring talks and workshops focused on professionalizing and supporting people who work in developer relations (which involves connecting platform and API providers with developer communities). As a cofounder of a makerspace in Seattle, for example, Clarissa focused on assembling a team with different and complementary skill sets (in hardware, software, and management), experiences, perspectives, and identities, and she focused on leveraging those team members' networks and skills to connect with local communities. And as an advocate for inclusivity in technology industries, Clarissa works to create online and in-person communities of support—be it a Slack channel for people of color in hardware and software industries around the world or a Women Who Code meetup in Seattle.

The focus on communities and their goals is also why Clarissa prefers *community strategy* to a term like *growth hacking*, though, again, community strategy can certainly include growth hacking. In addition to the resistance to the term *growth hacking* Clarissa has encountered from colleagues in software and hardware development (who are concerned about whom and what is being hacked), she also notes that growth is not always the desired or best outcome for the developer, provider, or the community. Community strategy instead emphasizes the localized nature of outcomes and the importance of tailoring both the nature of the engagement and the measure of that engagement's success to the community, rather than imposing a set of goals or assumptions.

The emphasis on strategy in the name "community strategist" highlights the skills involved in building relationships, connecting complementary differences, and localizing developer and community goals. Indeed, a community strategist cultivates a global network of people with diverse skills, identities, and experiences, covering a range of organizations, cultures, languages, and geographical locations, in order to be able to wield that network effectively for specific purposes—whether it is connecting a Polish data science company with niche US markets, or connecting a person of color who may feel alone in his workplace with a community of other people of color in working in technology. In other words, a community strategist works at and intervenes in boundaries by configuring and reconfiguring communities, which also involves configuring and reconfiguring rhetorical practices and goals, as we demonstrate in our analysis.

Furthermore, the tactics a community strategist employs are rhetorical and user-centric, and the community strategist, like technical communicators and user experience researchers, plays an important role in the user localization process. The product may no longer be in its initial development by the time the community strategist is involved, but the community strategist helps an organization anticipate and facilitate user localization processes, which, in turn, can lead to refining not only marketing and technical materials but also the product or service itself as well as organizational practices. Technical communication is important to community strategy, whether it is writing a DIY tutorial for a product to engage online communities or localizing web content for a niche market.

Likewise, user experience is important to community strategy: the community strategist's goal is to create a positive, useful first experience (rather than merely a first impression), and the strategist carefully creates environments and situations for that initial experience, drawing on rhetorical knowledge of the community. Like user experience (UX) researchers and technical communicators, community strategists intervene rhetorically in the complex nexus of markets, technologies, developers, and communities. Sarah Murray and Megan Sapnar Ankerson (2016) analyze the challenges faced by the developer of a lesbian dating app in balancing user preferences with funding demands. Specifically, lesbian users desired a distinctly queer and slow mode of temporality (not rushing to a hookup, in contrast to gay apps like Grindr), but the start-up world and capital providers demand quick pathways to traditional revenue generators like matching, chatting, and meeting up with other users. While Murray and Ankerson do not mention a community strategist in their analysis, the challenges they describe are precisely those that a community strategist is well positioned to navigate, along with UX researchers and technical communicators. As Claire Lauer and Eva Brumberger (2016) point out, rhetorical skills are as essential to user experience as creativity.

Finally, an ability to work empathetically and effectively across differences—not only race/ethnicity, gender, class, sexuality, language, culture, and ability, but also skill sets, goals, and situations—is at the heart of community strategy, much like technical communication and user experience. Social justice and inclusion advocacy are central to the work of community strategy. As a Filipino American woman who grew up in poverty in Oakland, California, Clarissa is aware of and strategically wields her embodiment of diversity in technology as a way not only of demonstrating the importance of inclusion but also as a way of supporting others who are marked as different. She draws on her own experiences of working across cultures and differences to help companies, organizations, and developers do the same, and key to this work is treating inclusion itself—like the communities, technologies, and goals—as a localized practice. And even when a client's goal is not explicitly to reach or include "diverse" communities, Clarissa's own commitment to cultivating diversity—in many different forms—in her networks and contacts means that a broader, more inclusive reach is embedded in her work, which can ultimately benefit both her client and the communities she connects.

Clarissa advocates for and practices inclusion both in the technology industry and in community access to technologies, and her commitment to social justice permeates her work as a community strategist. Central to her advocacy practice is continually localizing inclusion itself—specifically, the definitions of diversity and social justice outcomes. While there are certainly issues of diversity and social justice—for example, representation of women in technology industries—that transcend local circumstances, Clarissa emphasizes that the approach to inclusion should always be localized. In other words, "diversity" and "inclusion" are not static definitions we can begin with; rather, we must define "diversity" and "inclusion" in response to particular contexts and the bodies being marked. This is an ethical boundary-marking practice. Furthermore, while organizations may have representation from people of diverse backgrounds, identities, and abilities, this does not mean that those people are made to feel welcome; inclusion is an active localization practice that includes whether or not diversity and difference is explicitly named and in what ways, as well as whether or not the advocacy comes from a community, the community strategist, a client, or some combination of these. Key to this work is exploring local contexts and balancing one's own commitment to advocacy with the goals and commitments of the communities engaged, which, in turn, can lead to sustainable progress toward not simply describing but redressing inequities, as Natasha Jones and Rebecca Walton (2018) advocate.

As a community strategist, Clarissa recognized that one of the problems with diversity and access in technology industries is that the channels companies use to recruit employees, users, and communities are the "same old channels"—including, for example, predominantly white US universities, or predominantly male meetups or special interest groups. A community strategist can intervene in this feedback loop by including more channels to more communities, especially those underrepresented in technology industries. Clarissa leverages the diversity in her community relationships to make meaningful connections that include more voices, identities, experiences, and perspectives. Even when a company's explicit goals do not involve increasing diversity in its user communities, Clarissa connects her own, more diverse networks as part of her strategy work. In this way, Clarissa's reconfiguring of boundaries through a localized practice of diversity and inclusion advocacy can benefit both companies and communities.

Indeed, Clarissa taught me the importance of a "Show, don't just tell" approach to localizing and supporting inclusivity. As we discussed and reflected on Clarissa's work cofounding SoDo Makerspace and the fact that after she left, there were fewer women and people of color involved in the space, we realized that while the intention of the makerspace to be inclusive remained unchanged, what did change is that Clarissa herself was no longer prominently visible in the space to *show* diversity and inclusivity in practice. When Clarissa is in a position to make increased inclusion an explicit goal—for example, in her work organizing conferences like the DevRel Summit in Seattle—she is careful about how (or if) she explicitly names the diversity she is working toward. Since her goal was to recruit balanced representation of men and women at the DevRel Summit, she chose not to explicitly name it a women-focused conference, because she has found that naming the conference that way leads to low attendance by men. Instead, she made sure to advertise the event to channels that reached both women and men, and she recruited women and people of color to be speakers and leaders for the event.

As a result, women and men were nearly equally represented in the five hundred conference attendees, and a male developer relations professional who attended the event wrote in his review: "While the tech industry tends to be overwhelmingly white and male, the selection of presenters wasn't. When you factored in the panel compositions, there were more women on stage during the day than there were men, yet there was never a feeling that this was a conference about women or for women. It was simply a professional conference that just happened to have more women on stage. That was cool" (Bulmash 2016, n.p.). In her work with Women Who Code, Clarissa found that the fact that the word *women* is in the name of the group is a boundary mark that has sometimes led to sponsorships and partnerships that have felt more tokenizing than meaningful. Indeed, Clarissa's strategies for resisting tokenization remind me of decolonial queer feminist design scholar Ece Canlı's argument that decolonizing design involves delinking from "the humanitarian design endeavors that *other the others* further and replace a multiplicity of voices with tokenism and diversity" (Schultz et al. 2018, 98–99).

The potential for tokenization prompted Clarissa and her colleagues to begin articulating guidelines for meaningful relationships, which they began by highlighting the inclusive practices of a partner organization they hold in high esteem. At the same time, as we were analyzing this experience, Clarissa realized although she and her colleagues had successfully fostered diversity in gender and ethnicity, they had missed an opportunity to reach out to older audiences. In some ways, the conference was focusing its outreach on people who were already inclined to agree and have similar perspectives, while missing the experiences and different perspectives of diverse age groups. She realized that if the goal of a community strategist is to foster a self-sustaining community, then creating an ecosystem that is as inclusive as possible of different demographics and experiences is essential.

Just as fostering meaningful, inclusive diversity in demographics and experience is important to the sustainability of a just community, Clarissa emphasizes that mentoring is crucial to community strategy work. Some of this mentoring work is directly connected to the contracted work of a community strategist. To sustain the relationships and networks she materializes beyond her own direct involvement, Clarissa mentors organization and community members to carry on the work of strategically assembling and connecting human, technological, and material resources across cultures. Mentoring is particularly important in groups who want to be more inclusive and diverse but are not sure how to go about making meaningful and sustainable changes. If, for example, the goal is to include more women, more people of color, or more people with disabilities, then Clarissa emphasizes the importance of having women, people of color, and people with disabilities at the center of that strategy work. "Ask them how to reach out meaningfully and trust and support them," Clarissa advises, echoing the "nothing about us without us" ethos of disability scholars and activists (Charlton 1998). But at the same time, she also emphasizes the intersectional nature of diversity: it is never just gender, just race/ethnicity, just class, just dis/ability, just geography. Rather, it is the intersections of all of these, which means that including and listening to many voices and perspectives is crucial for finding resonances amid differences.

Prototyping (for) Connections

As an intermediary between designers/providers and user communities, Clarissa practices strategies recognizable to teachers and practitioners of rhetoric and writing: listening (Breuch 2001; Ratcliffe 2005), responsiveness (Long 2014), and audience analysis (Ross 2013), both for clients and communities. She prioritizes listening to and respecting the goals of communities, because meaningful engagement and support of communities is foundational to successful community strategy. Ultimately, her work involves localizing the goals of both communities and providers through careful listening, understanding, and connecting. Clarissa relies on the following heuristic for learning about the goals and interests of the people she meets:

- What brought you [here]?
- How do you know [person]?
- How did you hear about [event]?
- What do you want to get out of [event]?
- How can I help you?

Sometimes Clarissa moves through this heuristic fairly quickly, as in the case of a conversation with a potential user at a meetup. But when she is working across cultures, she emphasizes time and observation, in addition to listening, as key to generating meaningful cross-cultural, cross-community understanding. The last question, "How can I help you?" is how the community strategist begins to connect their understanding of a person's or community's needs or interests with the community strategist's own resources and the resources—human, technological, informational, infrastructural—in their networks of connections.

I have come to understand that Clarissa's community strategy heuristic is a way of prototyping connections with people, technologies, and resources. Clarissa brings together community strategy prototyping and physical prototyping, often on the laser cutter. For example, all in a day (in January 2018), Clarissa went from pitching hardware kits to a program at a local community college, to pitching a workspace at a local coworking space to her Makerologist, to pitching Makerologist ideas to wealthy potential investors at an elite Seattle social organization. At the first meeting at the community college, which I attended with Clarissa and Alex Cheker (of MyOpen3D), Clarissa first asked questions and listened to her potential clients, who worked with multiply marginalized and underrepresented students. Clarissa identified with what they were sharing and shared about her own experiences in college, when she was homeless and ultimately had to drop out. "But I wouldn't be where I am today if I hadn't had that experience," she added. Later, in the car ride to the next meeting, Clarissa told me that she doesn't always share that much about herself, but that her choice to share was based on what she learned from asking questions and listening first. After going on to pitch a coworking space in Impact Hub Seattle to some of her Makerologist colleagues, Clarissa then prepared for her meeting with the elite social club over coffee. She wondered aloud whether she should go by her apartment for a hat to cover her blue hair but decided against it.

A few days later, I caught up with Clarissa at the MyOpen3D workshop about her meeting with the elite social club. For that meeting, Clarissa said, she drew on her "past corporate self" (she previously worked as a project manager at a bank) and put on a blazer and pulled back her hair. As with her other potential clients that day, Clarissa asked questions and listened first. "That's how I figured out what to ask them for," she explained. The group latched on to the term *makerology* and began talking among themselves about the "makerology movement" (instead of the more commonly used "maker movement"), much to Clarissa's delight. "I just went with it!" she said. She then asked the group to consider putting up small "Makerologist" loans of $5,000 as a low-risk way of helping makers launch a project (with the support of the Makerologist agency), and the group was amenable.

They invited Clarissa and Makerologist to cohost an upcoming event, so at the MyOpen3D workshop, Clarissa was prototyping a small gift for attendees: a small token laser etched with the club's insignia.

Clarissa's prototyping process on one material option (plywood) spanned thirty minutes, which I filmed continuously on my iPhone, excluding the initial step of pulling the club insignia into a vector program and exporting it for the first time to the laser cutter. Clarissa went through three iterations on the laser cutter, troubleshooting speed and power settings on the laser cutter, as well as tricky toolpaths for the ornate insignia letters in the vector program. When I started filming, Clarissa was sitting at a table with her laptop, working in Inkscape, an open-source vector graphics program, to create a set of lines for the laser cutter to trace and cut. She had already tried one cut on the laser cutter and was attempting to correct mistakes she found in the first prototype. As she worked, she chatted with me and with Tony Loiseleur, who was standing nearby eating his lunch from a bowl.

"It's so funny how people like us—we're just so in love with the process," Clarissa remarked as she worked. "Not so much the other way around."

"We like details," Tony replied.

"I like Micah's quote on the making process," Clarissa continued. "He's like, making to me is very much like organic food: it's not so much about the destination but the journey." She laughed and added, "Which is kinda nice."

"That's a good one to take to life," Tony said. "It's not about the destination, because we all die."

Clarissa laughed. "Yeah, guess where the destination is?" She returned her focus to her work on her computer, humming to herself. After a few moments, she looked back at me, still filming on my iPhone, and laughed again. "You're recording and I'm totally doing it the slowest way possible."

I laughed and replied, "Well, it *is* about the process."

Over the next half hour, I watched as Clarissa went through two prototypes on the laser cutter, each time tweaking her toolpath (the instructions to the laser cutter about where and at what speed and power to make its cuts) to correct errors that were revealed when she examined a completed prototype. She cut the prototypes out side by side on the piece of plywood she was using to avoid wasting material and having to reset the material in the machine each time (Figure 8). Each time the laser finished cutting, Clarissa opened the lid and used a small pin to detach the cut portion from the piece of plywood. She took the cut portion back to the workspace next to her computer and continued to gently push the cut pieces out to see if

Figure 8. A laser cutter carries out Clarissa's instructions for a third prototype

the pieces she wanted to stay attached were still attached, and if the pieces she wanted to cut out came out cleanly.

"I think we got it!" she said to me after popping out the cut pieces of the third prototype, and she held the finished prototype up to my camera lens. "Third time's a charm."

Clarissa's prototyping on the laser cutter required time, patience, flexibility, troubleshooting, and willingness to try things. She brings the same dispositions to her work prototyping human connections—as well as sustaining and strengthening those connections. The following month (when I was back in Arizona), we were caught up over video conference and talked about a piece we'd both recently read about a marginalized community's work to support its members over decades. Clarissa noted that she felt both "pride and resilience in this work, but also sadness. Why do we have to fight so long for change? What do we need to change about our strategies and tactics?"

"Maybe we're preaching too much to the choir," she continued, echoing the advice she gave my students when she visited my digital rhetorics class at the University of Washington the day after the 2016 presidential election, when many of us were feeling at a loss about what to do next. That day, after listening to students share their reactions, Clarissa urged us to work for change within our reach by talking outside of our echo chambers. She returned to this strategy in our 2018 video chat. "We've got to change our rhetoric and change who we're talking to." Indeed, I've learned from Clarissa that making community—in and beyond the maker movement—means bringing a spirit of empathetic, human-centered pro-totyping to our networks and connections. As Clarissa later explained to me in a May 2019 conversation, "You need someone who is willing to take the time to look inside you, take the time to understand you, and take the time to help you make the connection." She also explained, "Like the process of making, you never really get it right the first time. But the more we take the time to understand and allow ourselves and others to make mistakes, the better equipped we become to handle (or design) anything." As a practitioner and teacher of writing and rhetoric, I find that Clarissa's approach to prototyping connections in relationships and 3D fabrications applies just as much to prototyping connections in rhetorical compositions across modalities, and I return to this in detail in the next chapter. But first, I conclude with a discussion of advice on making from people in this study that is inspired by Clarissa's community strategy work of inviting multiple perspectives.

Advice on Making

I have learned from the people I've met through SoDo Makerspace and Makerologist, as well as from scholarship on the maker movement, that there are many definitions of making, makers, and the maker movement itself. Different definitions of who counts as a maker and what counts as making come from different embodied, emplaced perspectives and rela-tionships. Different definitions of who counts as a maker and what counts as making also open up and foreclose different possibilities for different bodies. To illustrate and share these different perspectives, I asked people from SoDo Makerspace and Makerologist to share their advice on making, so that we can circulate that advice to people reading this book. Readers will note that the advice varies, as do the perspectives and positionalities of the advice-givers—not unlike the perspectives and positionalities of people in and beyond the global maker movement. After the advice from people in this study, I offer additional advice for researchers and teachers.

From Eric Renn, CEO of SoDo Makerspace

- My advice for what it takes to "make it" as a maker is to keep operating expenses lean and make use of the materials around you.
- The most valuable thing I've learned about making is that one can only learn so much by watching. Start by visiting a makerspace to see a machine in action, then get to work doing, if that space will teach you how to use the machine! In the beginning it's a little overwhelming, but if you choose a single tool and make as many things as possible with that tool, you'll be empowered to try more.
- Here are a few tips for getting started as a maker:

  - Pick a single-modality tool such as a laser cutter (subtractive, manufacturing/prototyping, computer-aided fabrication tool) or a 3D printer (three-axis, additive manufacturing machine).
  - Learn about one prototyping tool at a time. Give yourself three months of consistent (at least two to four hours a week) human-to-machine interaction and try as many things as possible with that tool. Try to use a lot of different materials and shapes.
  - Get started with someone else's files on the internet by visiting websites such as Thingiverse or Instructables.
  - Search Google for scalable vector graphics (.svg) for the laser cutter.
  - Explore stereo lithographic (.stl) files for 3D printing.
  - Once you understand the basics of a tool, learn to use computer-aided design graphic software (such as Inkscape) or 3D design web-based software (such as Tinkercad) to make the objects you envision.

- Makers can make the world a better place by sharing ideas, files and collaborating on a local community projects that solve a common problem. As a member or a volunteer anyone can capture the skills and experiences happening at a local makerspace and then archive those experiences by teaching classes, holding an event for a special interest meetup group, or sharing failures and outcomes on a global and unrestricted scale by posting archived videos on the internet.
- The future of makerspaces is the mobile workshop or mobile training facility. A static location can only reach so far in a local community. Makerspace collaborators that deliver tools and skills on the road where the entire makerspace is on wheels will result in a much wider range of educational outreach.

From Micah Summers, cofounder and director of the West Seattle Tool Library

- Advice for makers:

  - There's *always* multiple solutions to a problem.
  - Hey now! You're not a rock star, and that's OK.
  - Listen to the voice in your head trying to talk you out of things, then promptly shove it in a box for a few hours.

- Most valuable thing learned about making:

  - Making is the nebulous space connecting our minds, bodies, and the world around us. Its vastness is boundless in both depth and complexity.

- What it takes to "make it" as a maker:

  - Making it as a maker is a state of mind.
  - One can, with relative ease, bushwhack through fears of uncertainty, seeing a horizon beyond the land of biases.
  - One occasionally ponders if making is more about the journey than the destination.
  - They may discover that the net worth of their experiences and creative exercises can make a handmade solution far more valuable than one they could find in retail.

- What makers can do to make makerspaces and the world a better place:

  - Open your mind. Listen. Share. Volunteer.

- What the future looks like for makers and makerspaces:

  - In one word, *redonckulous.* Our society is struggling to keep up with our accelerating access to knowledge, tools, and resources along with ever-crumbling barriers to entry. It's getting pretty hard to imagine something you *couldn't actually make.*

From Clarissa San Diego, Founder and CEO of Makerologist

- Ask yourself first, "What type of maker do I want to be?" Do you want to be a hobbyist? Do you want to work for yourself? Do you have a product you want to create? Or maybe you don't know what exactly you want to do, but you do know you're curious about making. These aren't completely distinct categories, of course, but it's an important question to ask yourself. The foundational articulation of who you are and who you want to be can be what makes a maker, and it shapes how you do what you do.

- Part of understanding who you are as a maker is understanding your strengths and weaknesses. When you think of your strengths, which ones would you enjoy teaching others? And when you think of your weaknesses, which ones do you want to level up, and which ones are you OK with?
- It's important to have a clear sense of your strengths and weaknesses, of your own self, and of your bandwidth. Having this clear sense can help you avoid the biggest mistake a maker can make: simply working alongside others instead of working with others. Know who you are as a maker and what you can contribute to a project.

I share these different perspectives here (and throughout the book) for several reasons. I want to add my voice to those who emphasize that practices and definitions of "making" and "maker" are multiple, and those different practices and definitions have consequences for who may or may not identify as a "maker." I share these different perspectives—along with my own perspectives—as a way of illustrating the ways in which these stories are made in ongoing, dynamic relations with people, spaces, perspectives, and things.

I also share these different perspectives on making—some of which emphasize tools, some of which emphasize invention, some of which emphasize relationships—to highlight the differences made by the different emphases. These different emphases are different boundary-marking practices that, in turn, shape different practices of making (with 3D objects, with symbols, with words, with gestures, and more). A focus on tools shapes who can make (who has meaningful access to the tools?) and what can be made (what can the machine do? What can people afford to do with the machine?). A focus on invention, both in the rhetorical and in the entrepreneurial sense, likewise shapes who can make (who identifies as a maker? As an inventor?) and what can be made (what are the limits of creativity and imagination?). Both tool-focused and invention-focused approaches to making have value and seem to be common in the maker communities I have engaged, just as tool-focused and invention-focused approaches to rhetoric and writing have value and are common in classrooms. And finally, a focus on relationships also shapes who can make (in relation to which communities? Which other makers?) and what can be made (what do communities want? How do they work together to make things?). Such a relational focus can benefit makers of things, rhetoric, and writing in and beyond makerspaces—including, as I suggest in the next chapter, teachers and researchers.

CHAPTER SIX

Teaching

I came to this study of making and relational rhetorics in and beyond a makerspace from my positionality as both a researcher and teacher of writing and rhetoric. My positionality as a teacher piqued my curiosity about what I perceived as increasing uptakes of contemporary maker culture in the teaching of writing and rhetoric: from teaching 3D printing as a process of rhetorical composition (and documentation) to turning classrooms into makerspaces for multimodal compositions. My positionality as a teacher also shaped the questions I brought to the study and the connections I made in my observations of and conversations with people I met. And, in turn, observing how people learned and taught strategies for prototyping often sparked ideas for my own practice as a writer and for my practice as a teacher of writing and rhetoric.

During 2015, the first year of this study, I served as an assistant writing program administrator in my department at the University of Washington, so I was not in the writing classroom myself. I returned to the classroom in the spring quarter of 2016, when I was assigned to an upper-level undergraduate writing course in a newly established multimodal composition sequence. I had served on the committee to develop this sequence and was eager to pilot one of the new courses with a class design I called Rhetoric in the Making. In fact, the beginning of that committee work in late 2014 coincided with my introduction to the maker movement. The conversation I describe at the beginning of this book with a colleague during which I had to surreptitiously google the word *makerspace* was about models for multimodal composition, which I was seeking out and pondering as the committee began its work.

Given these beginnings, it is not surprising that what I learned in my study of making and rhetorics both shaped and was shaped by my practice of teaching writing and rhetoric. This chapter is a story of two iterations of that Rhetoric in the Making class at the University of Washington, one in spring 2016 and another in fall 2016. It is also the story of a collaborative research-design relationship with students from both iterations of the course that resulted in the publication of a coauthored article (Shivers-McNair et al. 2018). I was dwelling in the intersections of rhetorics and acts of making, and it was bound to show in my teaching. I embraced opportunities to understand how the nonlinear, relational, and (sometimes) disequilibrating practices of prototyping I observed and experienced in a makerspace might play out in a multimodal composition class. I also embraced opportunities to learn from and with students, just as I was also learning from and with people I met in a makerspace, about how we can make and teach rhetoric and writing together.

Therefore, just as previous chapters tell stories of how theories, method/ologies, and practices intersected in my experiences and relationships in the study, this chapter tells the story of how my experiences as a researcher intersected with my experiences as a teacher. I find that those two identities are often in dialogue with each other, which will not surprise readers in my areas of study—after all, composition studies in particular has historically been a "teaching subject," to borrow Joseph Harris's (2012) words—or readers in education and other disciplines that conduct research on teaching and learning. Throughout this book, I have told stories about making and relational rhetorics, and I've told stories about disequilibrium and spatial manipulations in rhetorical practices of making. And I've told stories about community and story making as both the starting point and end goal of making and rhetorics. I thread those concepts through the stories in this chapter to illustrate how my research and teaching experiences informed each other and to offer approaches and insights I learned from these intersections.

Making and Relational Rhetorics

My first iteration of the Rhetoric in the Making course was guided by scholarship on making and composition that focuses on the possibilities for multimodal and 3D composition (Craig 2014; Shipka 2011, 2016) and on opportunities to make rhetorical interventions in a culture where access to 3D fabrication is increasingly widespread (Sheridan 2010; Sherrill

2014). I called my course design Rhetoric in the Making because I wanted to emphasize both the processes of creating rhetorical compositions and the rhetorical work of composing across modalities and media. Ultimately, I wanted to guide my students through an experiential examination of discursive and nondiscursive forms of making as rhetorical interventions involving the relations of bodies (human and beyond) and material-cultural environments. But I did not want use the word *makerspace* to describe the class, nor did I want the class to be about the maker movement. I was reluctant to privilege the technologies of maker culture, specifically, when my goal was to engage students in practicing and accounting for writing as a form of making, alongside other forms of making. I agree with Jody Shipka (2011) that "it is crucial that we not limit our attention to a consideration of new media texts or to what the newest computer technologies make possible—or even make problematic—but attend to the highly distributed, complexly mediated, multimodal dimensions of all communicative practices" (29). While I can recognized the value in assigning a particular medium/mode (such as 3D printing) to all students, I was more interested in what would happen when students chose the media and modalities they worked in.

My decision to leave the choice of media and modalities (and projects) up to students was also grounded in my local context: the course I taught was in a multimodal composition sequence that is part of the undergraduate English major, though the course is also open to nonmajors and satisfies a university-required writing credit. Thus, the class positions English majors alongside engineering, business, science, communication, and fine arts majors. I saw this as an opportunity to recreate (and expand upon) one of the practices I admire most about makerspaces: bringing together makers with different expertises and encouraging collaboration among them. Thus, from the outset I encouraged students to draw on and expand their disciplinary, experiential, cultural, linguistic, and technical resources; to dwell in and design projects that resonated with their interests and concerns in and outside the academy; and to recognize each other as potential collaborators and resources.

As scholars like Diana George (2002), Jason Palmeri (2012), Cynthia Selfe (2009), Jody Shipka (2011), and Geoffrey Sirc (2003) have shown us, attending to the materialities of meaning making beyond words and texts has been part of the work of writing studies from its beginnings, if not part of its mainstream practices. And as Adam Banks (2011) and Angela Haas (2007) remind us, multimodal composing practices that may seem relatively new to our field, like remixing or even hypertext, have roots in the embodied rhetorical practices of Black, Indigenous, and People-of-Color communities. Building on these traditions, I embraced in the classroom, as I did in my approach to my study of making, an approach to rhetorics that encompassed more than human words and human intentions. Therefore, in my assignment prompts, I did not specify quantities of written (alphabetic) content or equivalent production of other media content. Rather, I framed benchmarks in terms of engaging rhetorical concepts and meeting rhetorical goals, and I worked with students to localize the scope, deliverables, and measurements of effectiveness of their particular projects. In the end, students produced more writing than the minimum amount specified by departmental requirements for a course fulfilling a writing credit, even as they also were engaged in other kinds of composing, including web design, sewing, crafting, cooking, videography, choreography, and data visualizations.

I acknowledge that while this worked well in this particular course context (students' projects were highly successful in meeting the expectations I set for the course, and students responded positively in course evaluations), in other contexts, more structure might be helpful. Still, my experiences as a teacher have led me to tend to err on the side of giving students more room to localize projects for specific goals and contexts within the parameters of course expectations. This was my attempt to renegotiate the boundaries of what and who can come to matter in my pedagogical design by creating as many opportunities as possible to attend to boundary marking in our unfolding relationships as a class and in students' relationships with the communities they engaged in their projects.

Disequilibrium in Teaching

These unfolding relations can lead both intentionally and unintentionally (from the perspective of individual humans) to experiences of disequilibrium in our collective and individual work. Rhetorical forces of disequilibrium—both as an inevitability and as an intentional practice of invention—are boundary markings that open up possibilities for some bodies and foreclose possibilities for others. In this way, disequilibrium can serve as a site not only for invention but also for intervention. (Indeed, students in the first iteration of Rhetoric in the Making, especially, endured my constant use of the styling *in(ter)vention*.)

As I was conceptualizing and reconceptualizing Rhetoric in the Making,

I was also experiencing and observing disequilibrium in my research. For example, the laser cutter fires resulting from the "ready, fire, aim" approach I observed in SoDo Makerspace drew my attention to sites of communication (or miscommunication) that might otherwise have been taken for granted or not well understood. Furthermore, while the departure of Lauren, a woman-identified volunteer, marked an absence of women-identified bodies in SoDo Makerspace for much of my fieldwork, her departure also marked an expansion in the design of this study. I began reaching out to other people who had moved on from SoDo Makerspace, a change that both expanded the scope of the study and continued to enrich my understandings of what I observed in SoDo Makerspace.

These observations from my research convinced me that it is important to pay attention to boundary-marking practices like these when we employ disequilibrium as a practice of teaching rhetorical invention. For example, Marc Santos and Megan McIntyre (2016) draw on Jody Shipka's work in advocating for asking students to work "outside the expectations and forms of established genres" in order to expand their "creative capacity, autonomy, and their ability to negotiate ambiguity" (n.p.). But like technologies and interfaces, disequilibrium itself—even as a pedagogical or invention strategy—is not neutral; it is inherently a political, differential, boundary-marking practice. Just as Kate Losse (2016) emphasizes that "failing fast" in Silicon Valley is not a universal experience but a privilege afforded primarily to white men with access to venture capital, failing fast in writing classrooms is entangled with difference and privilege. When we look at disequilibrium through an intersectional lens (Crenshaw 1989), we can consider the ways in which a failure or discomfort might not be experienced in the same way by everybody in a makerspace or a classroom. An experience of failure or discomfort that might benefit one person whose positionalities are relatively privileged could also be harmful or exclusionary for another person whose positionalities are less privileged in a space.

Furthermore, the problems in what Eric describes as a "bootstrapped" makerspace—run by a collective of people ranging from amateurs to experts, some self-taught and some formally trained—are often and perhaps not surprisingly what Horst Rittel and Melvin Webber (1974) describe as wicked problems, in the sense that there are, as Eric once said, "too many variables" (human and nonhuman). They are also wicked in the sense that the expertise required to (permanently) solve a problem sometimes exceeds the knowledge of the user, and in the sense that fixes sometimes lead to more problems. In a materialist sense, the problems are wicked (perhaps regardless of whether humans experience them as such) in that they involve an entanglement of interfaces among humans, nonhumans, time, materials, alphabetic and spoken languages, written and embodied knowledges, gestural and haptic interactions, and cultural and economic forces.

It seemed to me that the regulars in SoDo Makerspace tended to work with, rather than against, these wicked entanglements by treating both problems and solutions (however temporary) as "open source." I mean that not only in the sense of open-source hardware and software (so prized in the maker movement and in DIY culture) but also in a metaphorical sense. As Clarissa San Diego explained to me, an open-source approach to making involves "understanding that when things go wrong, there's a process to figure out how to make it right." And that process almost always involves distributed, shared knowledge that spans written, verbal, gestural, embodied, digital, analog, human, and nonhuman forms. In other words, to become a "maker" seems to be as much about learning through failure as it is about learning from codified knowledge, and as much about seeking out "open source," distributed knowledge as it is about possessing individual knowledge.

These practices resonated with my understandings of teaching. Richard Marback (2009) argues that composition studies has failed to account for the wickedness of design (which he connects with rhetoric) by "isolating the 'individual action' of the designer from the agency of artifacts" (408). Marback is referring specifically to Gunther Kress's focus on a composer who agentively navigates the affordances of various media, but I would extend Marback's argument to the use of individual reflections for teaching and assessing the wicked problem of design. What Shaun Slattery (2005) calls mediation, or what Marback calls design, is a wicked problem in a more than human sense, in that "agency" is a complicated matter that extends beyond a single human writer/rhetor/designer/maker.

Scholars like Brenton Faber (2002) have argued that agency also extends beyond structure-versus-individual-agency models that suggest individuals can combat structural forces if they work hard enough or possesses the right skills. Such skills also include "literacies," as Anne Frances Wysocki and Johndan Johnson-Eilola (1999) point out in their critique of the neoliberal promise of literacy as mobility. Rather, agency is part of the negotiations and relations among a complex array of humans, things, and meanings in time and space. And, as I have argued throughout this book, in my more than humanist but still human-centered view, "giving objects their due" (Marback 2008) in a more than human view of agency needs to be complemented with intersectional approaches that account for the ways in which some humans are still not given their due—in makerspaces, in classrooms, and more.

As a teacher of rhetoric and writing, my goal is to prepare students to intervene in rhetorical situations and wicked problems and to write in complex academic and professional situations. Instead of understanding "skills" as individual to a singular writer/rhetor and "affordances" as compartmentalized to media and genre, I find it more productive to think of these things as a relational, multidimensional field of rhetorical forces, bringing together intersectional and distributed understandings of rhetoric and agency. But this shift in understanding also requires a shift in how grading works. I can't think of rhetorical work as a relational, multidimensional field of forces but still grade as if skills are individual to a singular writer/rhetor. I try to create safe spaces for productive disequilibrium and encourage students to engage entangled failures productively in ways that account for privilege and different experiences of "failure." I try to recognize the importance of time, to understand problems and their solutions as entangled (or wicked) and "open source." And I try to be mindful of the intersectional, distributed processes of embodiment—including who and what comes to matter and who and what is excluded from mattering—involved in solving problems.

In the iterations of the Rhetoric in the Making course, this meant creating space for nonlinear approaches to composing processes. To foster this approach, I designed low-stakes requirements for the weekly studio assignments in order to encourage students to explore and take risks as they worked toward the final project. I also opened the possibilities for the final project to include a series of "failed" prototypes, or a refined low- or mid-fidelity prototype, or a high-fidelity prototype or even a finalized product. In this way, I tried to recreate another condition of makerspaces that I admire, which is a disposition of trying to learn from failure (or disequilibrium).

This disposition involves facing the discomfort and disappointment of failure (or even a string of failures) without being overwhelmed by it, in ways that resonate with Kelly Myers's (2016) discussion of *metanoia*, which we read together and discussed in the class. This orientation to disequilibrium also involves being willing to let go or move on (and, conversely, knowing when to commit resources to revision and development), and understanding failure as an opportunity to learn from mistakes or reenvision goals, purposes, or expectations. And just as disequilibrium—finding oneself in a system imbalance, or actively disrupting a system—could be an invention and innovation strategy in SoDo Makerspace, ethically managed disequilibrium in a learning environment can also be generative, as Santos and McIntyre (2016) argue.

Instead of a more or less linear or recursive process of composing in which an initial draft must be carried out to a final version, even if heavily revised, I observed in SoDo Makerspace nonlinear processes of rapid prototyping in which many barebones prototypes were generated without the expectation that all (or even most) of them should be developed or revised. I tried to recreate this—to the extent it's possible, given the vastly different institutional contexts—in my Rhetoric in the Making class. The course structure moves through a more or less linear model of composing concepts and strategies in rhetoric, design, and professional communication. But even though the concepts are introduced in this way, the weekly assignment prompts encourage students to explore a nonlinear process, including coming to terms with failed prototypes, in weekly studio sessions.

For example, even as we move from discussing and modeling research as an empathetic practice one week to discussing and modeling empathetic and accessible design the next week, students can (and do) continue exploring empathetic research in their studio activity for that next week. I found that in many cases, it took weeks of building trust with students for them to take me at my word when I said that failing can be as valid and useful as not failing, and when I said that not every prototype has to be revised or carried forward. I made a point of modeling and fostering a spirit of generosity toward all work, especially as some students seemed to be moving forward with compositions and others found themselves back at the drawing board. I found that students not only adapted to a wide range of composing stages each week (not to mention the wide range of media, goals, and expertise), but also became genuinely invested in their classmates' work and processes, which they demonstrated in collegial in-person interactions and wrote about in their reports and course evaluations.

But even as I worked to create safe spaces for risk-taking and failure in the scope of my course, I talked frankly with students about the ways in which "failing fast" is not a neutral or universal concept, but is bound up with privilege and context, as a 2016 *New York Times* editorial by Kate Losse that we read together argues so well. While some students are initially uncomfortable with and even resistant to the nonlinear composing process in the course, all students, in the end, took me up on my provision that the final project need not be "finalized" in the sense they might have initially envisioned. But, as we are all aware, the realities of other composing situations—in other classes, and in various community and work settings—do not always allow for such flexibility with timelines and expectations. Therefore, we also talk about how students can carve out spaces for themselves to take risks, let go of and learn from failures, and seek out feedback, even when the formal structure of a class or work setting does not provide such spaces.

Spatial Manipulations

Our work together to navigate and leverage disequilibrium involved complex relations of factors (human and nonhuman, discursive and nondiscursive) that were similar to what I was observing and experiencing in my research on making. The kaleidoscopic, endlessly looping, and interconnected movements of a 3D-printed spatial manipulation fidget toy became a way of understanding the complex relations and boundary markings in a makerspace and in a classroom. To return to the words of Cynthia Selfe (2009), students, like people in a makerspace, "need a full quiver of semiotic modes from which to select" to engage in "wickedly complex communicative tasks" (645). But just how we do that in rhetoric and writing classrooms is (and has been) contested. A current school of thought often described as postpedagogy argues, as Paul Lynch (2011) explains, that there is not a single true pedagogical approach and that pedagogy is what happens after class, rather than before (95). Like Steph Ceraso, Matthew Pavesich, and Jeremy Boggs (2019), I view the complexity highlighted by postpedagogical theory as an invitation to move beyond a binary of "absolute chaos" or "deterministic success" (n.p.). In this sense, postpedagogy is perhaps the most similar approach to what I observed in SoDo Makerspace, in that its advocates emphasize creativity and personalized instruction and intervention over standardized curriculum.

But there is also a tendency in postpedagogy and other design-based approaches (and in makerspaces, for that matter) to treat creativity as a neutral force or as a habit to be cultivated. The making and telling of the stories in a makerspace and in classrooms reminds me, however, that creativity is not merely a choice or habit of a single individual. In the case of Tony's work to make space for himself (and for visitors) in SoDo Makerspace, making involves the complex relations of humans, things, meanings, and spaces in ways that exceed individual intentionality and in ways that mark some bodies as more "useful" or more "maker" than others. Likewise, in a classroom, Ceraso, Pavesich, and Boggs argue that "it is critical to consider how race, gender, and other aspects of students' intersectional identities (e.g., disability, socio-economic status, etc.) might affect the inclusivity of a design-oriented learning environment" (n.p.). Therefore, I take a relational approach to the design of pedagogy, including evaluation of student work, as a way for accounting for complex relations and mitigating boundary-marking practices.

Just as I initially conceptualized my qualitative research approach as 3D interviewing, I initially conceptualized my approach to evaluating student work as 3D assessment, not only because it triangulates students' self-assessments, my assessment of their rhetorical skills, and audience-specific usability measures, but also (and most importantly) because it contextualizes rhetorical work in terms of 3D bodies in 3D, dynamic environments. And as was the case with my approach to research, I have since come to think of my approach to evaluating student work more broadly as multidimensional and relational. In the iterations of the Rhetoric in the Making course, the approach includes not only the way the final projects were assessed, but also the weekly studio sessions where students were constantly sharing, modeling, testing, exploring, explaining, and getting feedback on their work in progress.

My approach is, at least in part, a response to conversations in multimodal composition about the complexity of composing and transferring knowledge across media and modalities. As exciting as multimodal and new media composing can be for expanding how we and our students write and engage in rhetoric, we need to be careful about how we approach that work. Richard Marback (2009) argues that multiliteracy/design/multimodal approaches have thus far failed to account for the wickedness of composing and design by treating media as "affordances" to be manipulated by an agentive designer-writer-rhetor, rather than as forces exerted on the composing process (408), and by subordinating the logics of nonalphabetic compositions to the print-based logics of argument (410). Therefore, caution is needed in making claims about "knowledge transfer" between alphabetic media and nonalphabetic media, particularly when teachers and researchers rely on verbal and textual reflections to assess that transfer. And similar caution is needed in our approach to assessing multimodal/multimedia compositions.

My work is indebted to and builds upon the work of Jody Shipka (2011), who argues for "requiring that student assume responsibility for describing, evaluating, and sharing with others the purposes and potentials of their work" through documents like a statement of goals and choices (112–113). I do worry that emphasizing reflections on learning and process might lead me to treat those reflections as representations of a process, rather than as themselves a meaning-making process constrained by the teacher-student relationship. Just as I believe that reflexivity alone cannot substitute for ethical interventions and responsibility to the participants in my research, I believe I ought not position students' reflections as substitutes for responsibility to the embodied, material-discursive rhetorical effects of their work.

Therefore, just as my goal in developing the 3D interview method (which I now think of as relational knowledge-making) was to account for the co-constituting relations of words, gestures, spatial relations, bodies, time, and environments (rather than privilege verbal or written reflections), my goal in my approach to evaluating student work is to honor the dynamic, entangled, and distributed ways we make rhetorical compositions that matter. When I initially set out to adapt my 3D interviewing strategy developed for this study to a classroom practice, I considered the following questions:

- How can we teach writing alongside—and entangled with—other ways of composing without subordinating those other ways to the logics of traditional "writing"?
- Can we assess students' rhetorical dexterity across media without relying solely or primarily on written, individual reflections?

This last question is taken up in the edited collection *A Rhetoric of Reflection* (2016), in which J. Elizabeth Clark provocatively compares e-portfolios to selfies, noting that they are in many ways detached from contexts and that they are "an opportunity for the audience to make meaning of the image," which makes them an "anti-self-reflection" (164). And while Clark ultimately positions reflection as an antidote to that disconnect and as a dispositional practice that can transcend specific media, I am less convinced that the fracturing of contained, individual, medium-specific knowledge that Clark considers a disconnect is necessarily a problem.

I was struck by the distributed nature of knowledge and meaning making in SoDo Makerspace, and it led me to wonder what it would mean to focus on immersing students in entanglements and distributions of knowledge, instead of holding them individually accountable for skills through individual reflections or other performances. What if—to extend Rebecca

Nowacek's (2011) work—what we call "transfer" is as much about the integration of writers/makers (human and more than human) into a network as it is about individual humans integrating skills or knowledge across contexts (or technologies or media)? Furthermore, that process of integration almost always involves distributed knowledge that spans written, verbal, gestural, embodied, digital, analog, human, and nonhuman forms. To become a "maker" or even an "expert" seems to be as much (if not more so) about seeking out this "open source" distribution as it is about possessing individual knowledge.

To evaluate distributed, entangled, dynamic making as such, we need distributed, entangled, dynamic means of assessment. In my approach, this means distributing assessment (in the form of responses and reactions to work) across bodies, space, and time. The physical, digital, and temporal spaces of the classroom are saturated in low-stakes, ongoing, multiperspective feedback: from me, from classmates, from intended audiences/users of the work, from self-assessment (that can and often does include reflection). It also means that feedback and assessment are necessarily dynamic and therefore negotiable: I teach students to actively and rhetorically solicit useful feedback on their particular projects/process stages from me and from their peers and intended audiences/users.

And my approach to assessment also involves sharing the work of developing localized effectiveness measures with students and their intended audiences/users. Students draw on their understandings of rhetoric, design, usability testing, and feedback to develop effectiveness measures for their final projects by which their projects can be assessed on their own terms and students can demonstrate rhetorical skills within the contexts, time frames, media/modalities/languages, intended audiences/users, and goals of their specific projects. The balance of written, verbal, visual, aural, gestural, and 3D forms of meaning-making involved in students' deliverables and effectiveness measures is therefore localized, rather than stipulated upfront by me.

My undergraduate student coauthors and I discuss this dimensional, multilayered approach to assessment in detail in our article (Shivers-McNair et al. 2018). Here, I will briefly describe two examples offered by two of my coauthors, Hanh Mai and Joy Phillips. For Hanh, localizing effectiveness meant combining a pole-dancing routine she choreographed with a guide she developed for our class community on how to encounter and respond to pole dancing as art using rhetorical concepts. She used digital video and slides, as well as a printed handout, to present this work to her classmates, and she created a web page that also included an account of her past process, present stage, and future plans for her work. Joy, who had been prototyping a mobile app for fellow commuters, decided to stop working on the free app-design platform she'd been using for low-fidelity prototypes because she was increasingly frustrated with its limitations and increasingly realizing (as she had been teaching herself coding along the way) that she wanted to commit to building the app from the ground up. In her presentation to her classmates, she offered a narrative of her design and prototyping process (supplemented with digital artifacts, including a QR code for classmates to scan with their smartphones and demo the app prototype as they listened to her). She also shared with us her newly formed plans—as a result of her composing process and work on the app—to double major in English and informatics and to return to her commuter app as a future project in a design course. Both Hanh and Joy demonstrated rhetorical skills that were highly responsive to and localized for specific contexts, users, goals, media, modalities, and time frames. As Sharon Crowley (1999) has argued, the work of boundary negotiation—what and who count, what and who matter—is rhetorical, and by negotiating the terms by which their work is assessed with me, with their intended audiences/users, and with their own evolving goals, students are doing rhetorical work.

Stories and Community

Stories like Hanh's and Joy's were crucial to the work that happened in the iterations of Rhetoric in the Making and in the collaborative process of writing about Rhetoric in the Making with students. Stories became a method/ology for relational knowledge-making in my study, and it's no coincidence that stories—particularly as a design strategy—also became a method/ology for relational knowledge-making in my teaching practice and in my collaborative writing with students. And just as stories were an intersection point between my research and teaching, so was design. Perhaps not surprisingly, "design" was a word I heard often in my observations of and interactions with people in my study, from designing prototypes, to designing machine maintenance instructions, to designing communities. Eric Renn, CEO of SoDo Makerspace, kept a copy of the Stanford d.school's *Make Space* (Doorley and Witthoft 2012), which offers collaborative design strategies that emerged from the d.school's own makerspace (one of the early models of the contemporary makerspace in the United

States). Makerspaces are design-oriented spaces, as people imagine, collaborate on, prototype, and test their designs.

Relatedly, scholar-teachers in rhetoric, composition studies, and technical and professional communication emphasize design as a rhetorical practice. Since Richard Marback (2009) described a turn to design in composition studies, scholars like James Purdy (2014) and Carrie Leverenz (2014) have engaged with design thinking as a rhetorical and instructional strategy in composition studies. Ceraso, Pavesich, and Boggs (2019) advocate for "a design-centric approach to teaching that accounts for and is based in experience" (n.p.). Technical and professional communication has engaged with design through practices of user-centered design (Johnson 1998), UX design (Lauer and Brumberger 2016), and human-centered design (Walton 2016), as well as design thinking (Bay, Johnson-Sheehan, and Cook 2018). Across these areas and practices, design—like rhetoric—is an audience-focused practice that is important not only for students to learn, but for teachers to hold themselves responsible. As Douglas Eyman (2009) argues, "Curricular design is all too often enacted through a systems-design, rather than a user-centered, framework. We know what skills and rhetorical tools we want students to take with them from our classes, but we often ascribe these outcomes from our own understandings of usefulness and appropriate function" (222). In other words, we need understandings of usefulness that go beyond the teacher-designer-administrator's understandings of usefulness and center the perspectives of humans who use and are impacted by the pedagogical design, including and especially students.

Importantly, though, we need not only to pluralize perspectives within design, but also to locate the Western epistemology that underpins dominant definitions of design, and to pluralize epistemologies and practices of design. As Mahmoud Keshavarz argues,

> [It is] urgent to consider whose design (i.e. from what time and position and from where) has made and sustained the current hegemonic order . . . Think, for example, of the Western notion of design as a task of "problem-solving." This idea assumes a universal truth in addressing the complexity of the world as a series of problems to be solved. Moreover, it assumes the position of center for itself as given, and approaches other epistemologies from that given center, trying at best to collaborate with or at worst to assimilate them. (Schultz et al. 2018, 92)

To resist such universalizing and assimilating practices, Pedro Oliveira argues that decolonizing design is necessarily "a project of incompleteness, of persistently un-learning and re-learning to see the world" (Schultz et al. 2018, 94). And such persistent un- and relearning requires that "we move beyond inquiring who is offered a 'seat at the table' (to use Solange Knowles' language; Knowles 2016) but also the very terms used to set this 'table'" (94).

Oliveira's orientation to strategic incompleteness brings me (back) to stories—particularly in the form of narrative inquiry as articulated by Natasha Jones. Jones (2016) explains that "narrative inquiry can be used as a tool that engages feminist perspectives in a critical manner, providing researchers with rich data that has the ability to call into question existing knowledge, voices and silence, and perceptions" (479–480). Jones argues, furthermore, that narrative inquiry is not merely a descriptive tool, but also a strategy for design. User experience researchers and designers often create scenarios, or stories about human-users and how they might interact with a design, to hold designers responsible for creating things that are responsive to human-users (or audiences). And while often these scenarios combine the results of qualitative research into representative archetypes (or personas), Jones argues that scenarios are better used as an opportunity to bring in the real stories of real people—and especially those who are often not imagined as the "typical" or "ideal" user:

> Allowing often marginalized users' voices through narrative inquiry scenarios, and being aware of critical silences embedded in design and the design process, can promote designer-participant reflexivity, reflection, and positionality in the design process, encouraging genuine engagement and dialogue between researchers and participants and allow for more inclusive and equitable design. (481)

In other words, Jones argues for a strategically incomplete approach to personas and scenarios that resists a well-intentioned jump from individual people's perspectives to a "representative" user and, instead, preserves and acts upon the stories of otherwise marginalized people, both in voices and silences.

What might such an approach to narrative inquiry look like in the practice of pedagogical design? For me, it means telling stories and creating space for those stories to inform design—and that must include questioning the assumptions of "design" itself. For example, while I was teaching the first iteration of the course in spring 2016, I was inspired by my students' stories and practices of research and design work on accessibility for people with disabilities, as well as the Accessible Syllabus project at Tulane (Womack et al. n.d.), to make my own course materials more accessible and inclusive. I incorporated accessible design features (sans serif fonts, text that can be manipulated by screen readers, lower contrast in color pairings, a variety of visual and design elements instead of just long blocks of text, and alt-text and captions for images), as well as inclusive language (invitational rather than mandatory) and policy (presenting ways to accommodate needs and offering flexibility). In turn, when I shared the syllabus with students in the second iteration of the course in fall 2016, I told the story of how my rhetorical design choices were inspired by past students' work, as a way of acknowledging past work, inhabiting a shared present, and opening up future possibilities for me to learn from my students.

In addition to asking students to listen to and be informed by the stories of the communities with whom they were designing rhetorical compositions (for their projects in the course), I also made stories were the central work of our class time. For example, we held weekly studio sessions in which students shared stories of their in-progress work with each other. These sessions were a staple of both iterations of the course, and in both sections I invited students to envision different storytelling formats and configurations for our weekly studio sessions, which led to changes in the format that occurred toward the end of both iterations of the course. In the first iteration of the class (spring 2016), I scheduled the studio sessions for the second hour of each class period, meaning that (since our class met for two hours, two days a week) half the students shared their stories one class period, and the other half shared their stories the next class period, in any given week. The first class period hour each day was spent discussing and synthesizing readings and concepts. My rationale for this was, in retrospect, more system-centered design than user-centered design. I thought having the discussions and studio sessions back-to-back might create more cross-pollination between the two. And to further mix things up, I had a rotating studio schedule, so that students weren't stuck always presenting stories on the first day or the second.

However well-intentioned this system was in my teacher-designer mind, the system was often confusing for student-users in practice. I adhered closely to a gallery format for the storytelling sessions (three simultaneous presentations given three times, with the presenters stationed in three corners of the room and the audiences rotating among the presenters), because this was a format I had used in teaching public speaking that worked well as a low-stakes, practice-and-feedback format. But this, too, had its weaknesses, because (as students helped me realize) the goals of practicing delivering a speech are not the same as the goals we had for our studio sessions, which was to tell stories to help each other think through the usability of widely varying projects. And though I solicited feedback on the format throughout the course, it was mainly in terms of time parameters. It wasn't until the last studio session of the spring 2016 course that we changed the format entirely to better accommodate more meaningful storytelling.

In the second iteration of the class, in response to feedback from students in the first iteration, I changed the schedule: the first day of class each week was discussion day, and the second day of class each week was the studio day. This eliminated many headaches. I started again with the gallery format, and I held onto it for several weeks—which was still several weeks too long. We changed the format for the last few studio session to small group storytelling and discussion spaces, and this, I learned from my students, was by far the most productive session. This, in turn, led me to design studio sessions as self-selected, small-group, storytelling and discussion spaces for future iterations of the course that I taught at the University of Arizona.

Centering stories in the work of the class (however imperfectly) functioned as a localized practice of responsibility for our making practices at every step. In all the iterations of this class I have taught, we discuss how writing stories can help us be responsible and intervene ethically and effectively. One such way is reflective or metacognitive writing/thinking/speaking intended for the writer's own use as a means of rhetorical knowledge-making, which Kathleen Yancey (2016) describes as an approach characteristic of a third generation of reflection in writing studies. Anis Bawarshi (2010) advocates for this approach as a means to "delay and, as much as possible, interrupt the habitual uptakes long enough for students to examine critically their sources and motivations" and "consider what is permitted and what excluded by these uptakes" (201). In other words, creating pedagogical space for telling stories about the processes and choices of design and composing can, in turn, help students pause to interrogate the assumptions they make about genres, language, and people in their composing and design practices. Natasha Jones and Rebecca Walton (2018) argue, similarly, that as a pedagogical tool, narratives can enable critical insights through reflexivity. These insights can shape students' understandings of themselves as people and as professionals, as well as their ability to perceive relations of power that structure and operate in social contexts (Blyler 1995). Further, the reflexivity enabled by narrative is useful for considering what actions to take and the ethical merit of those actions, particularly when the production of narratives is interwoven with discussion. (247)

I invited these reflexive narratives in the form of weekly informal reports (written or delivered in audio and/or visual format) in which students shared stories of their ongoing choices, questions, and concerns about their work in progress with me and solicited feedback. Some students incorporated narrative accounts into the making of their project-specific effectiveness measures (as illustrated in Hanh's and Joy's stories). Stories became an invaluable, multimodal, multidimensional, and relational strategy for accounting for navigating design choices at the level of pedagogical design and at the level of students' projects.

Crucially, as I learned from my work with Clarissa San Diego (who also facilitated sessions of the Rhetoric in the Making class), stories are not only a descriptive practice; they are also an active, relational process of building community. In other words, in order to create safe spaces for encountering and leveraging disequilibrium through complex unfolding relations, we have to start with creating community. While I was teaching the iterations of Rhetoric in the Making, this meant fostering spaces of understanding and trust, which often happened through the continual telling of and listening to stories about projects and experiences in the class. These community foundations were important for the process of collaborating with self-selected student volunteers from both iterations of the class to write about our experiences in Rhetoric in the Making, beginning in early 2017.

Indeed, just as stories were central to my collaboration with Clarissa, stories were central to my collaboration with eight (then) undergraduate students who coauthored an article with me about Rhetoric in the Making: Joy Phillips, Alyse Campbell, Hanh Mai, Alice Yan, John Forrest Macy, James Wenlock, Savannah Fry, and Yishan Guan (Shivers-McNair et al. 2018). I learned from my collaboration with Clarissa that coauthoring is not only a way of fostering responsibility and making visible the shared labor of knowledge making, but it is also a way of building and sustaining community. This inspired me to write *with*, rather than *about* my students in our collaborative experience, analysis, and (re)design of pedagogy. Building on the foundation of storytelling that we established during our work together in the iterations of Rhetoric in the Making, we started the process of writing about and analyzing our experiences in the course by writing narratives. Each of us told the story of our experiences, and then we read each other's stories and together created metastories (stories about our individual stories) to help us understand the relationships among our experiences, particularly since our stories came from two iterations of the course.

In our first draft of the article we wrote together, however, we defaulted back to an IMRAD structure (Introduction, Methods, Results, Analysis, Discussion) that is often used in social science research writing. We also decided to blend our individual narratives together (and move them into third-person voice) so that we could organize the pieces of our stories thematically (i.e., a collection of examples about students' experiences with the studio sessions I describe above). At the time, this seemed to be a way to further structure our stories and metastories by using an organizational system with which our readers would be familiar. But as we learned from the peer review process, the IMRAD structure ultimately worked against our story-based approach. By trying to emphasize the data itself over the ways in which we actively cocreated the data, we flattened the dynamics of our collaboration and created an uneven voice throughout the piece.

One of the reviewers suggested we consult a 1999 *Computers and Composition* article by Pamela Takayoshi, Emily Huot, and Megan Huot as a model for a narrative-based structure for collaborative writing between a teacher-researcher and students. In my preliminary search for models of approaches to collaborating with undergraduate writers in rhetoric and composition I had found fewer resources than I'd hoped, though the ones I did find were helpful (particularly Hawisher et al. 2004). But I'd missed this piece, and when I pulled the article to read and share with my coauthors, I was struck by a passage that resonated strongly with my experiences co-making knowledge with the people in my research study:

> Although the stories included here, identified as Meghan's or Emily's might appear to be Emily and Meghan's sole contribution to the writing of this article, this was not the case. The stories are separate because they recounted the girls experiences, and we felt they captured best these experiences when written by the individual involved. The rest of the text was produced collaboratively the three

of us sitting around the computer, from organizing ideas in the drafting stages to composing sentences in the proofreading stage. Although we hope readers will hear the three different voices in this article, as any writing teacher knows, in a collaborative project, it is impossible to pinpoint exactly where one authors' ideas end and another's begins; our processes of thinking and writing, like those of any other coauthors, have fed into one another and triggered in us responses we would not have arrived at on our own. (Takayoshi, Huot, and Huot 1999, 92–93)

I realized that the practices I was employing in my collaborative writing on making could and should apply to my practices of writing with students. I discussed this model with my coauthors, and we agreed to try it in our revision. Both we and our editors were pleased with the result. In the published version of the article, we follow Takayoshi, Huot, and Huot's example and acknowledge the blending of our voices in the framing and connective tissue of our article, and we return to named, first-person narratives in the body of the article.

By not only telling stories but also making visible the dynamics through which those stories were made, our stories invite readers into our experiences and account for the making of knowledge through the relationships among a teacher and students. Thus, I learned the importance of stories in my collaboration and relationships with students, as I was also learning the importance of stories in my collaborations and relationships with people in the maker movement. I hope that these stories about the importance of stories can, in turn, invite readers into the experiences and relations through which the method/ologies and stories in this book were produced. I also hope that they can open up possibilities for applying and adapting relational approaches to knowledge making across contexts—in makerspaces, in classrooms, and beyond.

Conclusion

Futures

In September 2017, I caught up with Richard Albritton at the Seattle Mini Maker Faire, where he was going back and forth between the SoDo Makerspace booth and the Makerologist booth. Richard already knew, as Eric Renn (CEO of SoDo Makerspace) had shared with me earlier that same day, that SoDo Makerspace would not renew its lease when it came up the following year. Because he was involved in SoDo Makerspace from the beginning, I asked Richard what he thought about the possibility of the end of the space (at least as we knew it). He acknowledged that any time humans are trying to work together and build new things, there are challenges. "But in the maker movement there's no road map, so it's harder," he added.

A month later, the US locations of TechShop, an influential chain of makerspaces that many looked to as a model, closed and filed for bankruptcy, as I describe in Chapter 4. In 2018, the same year that SoDo Makerspace closed, another Seattle makerspace—the feminist makerspace described by Sarah Fox, Rachel Rose Ulgado, and Daniela Rosner (2015)—also closed. And yet another Seattle makerspace changed its business model to commissioned orders and fee-based consultations only. In 2019, Maker Media (which published *Make: Magazine* and managed maker faires worldwide) went out of business and was reconfigured as a member-funded organization intended to keep the magazine and maker faire brand running. I don't mean to suggest that all these closures and changes were for the same reasons, or that closures always equate to failures. I do think that these changes in the local and national makerspace ecosystem invite us to look beyond the model of a particular makerspace and toward the dynamic relations and ventures that bring people in, out of, and beyond makerspaces. Indeed, in the case of SoDo Makerspace, its closure might be viewed not only as an endpoint for a particular space and set of relations, but also as a launch point for new configurations and possibilities.

Clarissa San Diego, who also was a cofounder of SoDo Makerspace, founded Makerologist in 2017 with several other alumni of SoDo Makerspace. Another alumnus of SoDo Makerspace started a new makerspace, Seattle Makers, in 2017. And when I caught up briefly with both Richard and Eric over email in May 2019, both acknowledged that their experiences at SoDo Makerspace had created new professional opportunities for them. Richard, who had gone on to work at Seattle's Living Computers: Museum + Labs, told me via email in 2019 that his time at SoDo Makerspace "helped me get to the place I am at today doing exactly what I wanted to do." Eric began work in January 2019 as the sales engineer for D.A. International Group, a company a few doors down from where SoDo Makerspace was located and with whom Eric had collaborated (as CEO of SoDo Makerspace) to incubate start-ups and produce their designs. Eric told me via email that "this position has validated the prototyping skills and network of Makers I've acquired over the past five years and now I'm able to tap into the huge network of hardware startups as a Sales Engineer Professional."

I would add that SoDo Makerspace—and, more importantly, my relationships with the people I met there—had a launching effect on me, too. I have come a long way from when I first visited SoDo Makerspace and met Eric in February 2015 and struggled to answer his question, "So, what do you want to make?" The things I have learned and written about and presented about from SoDo Makerspace and from the makers I met there in the last several years have created opportunities for me and shaped my own career path. From the people in this book, and from my time in SoDo Makerspace during its four-year life span, I learned not only about making and rhetorics in a makerspace, but also about how important it is to trace making and rhetorics beyond a makerspace. In this last section of the book, I reflect on the affordances and constraints of my four-year study and the possibilities for continuing and new research directions it has opened for me.

My study was initially designed to examine a phenomenon with which I was unfamiliar: a makerspace. In tracing how people, machines, ideas, objects, and communities are made to matter (or not), I recognize and account for my own relationship to the people, things, and spaces I describe, and to the making of knowledge in these stories. Because this is a case study limited to a maker community in Seattle, I do not intend to generalize from these stories to make sweeping claims about the larger maker movement or about the extent to which SoDo Makerspace is representative of makerspaces. In this way, I locate both the reliability of my study in its account of entangled knowledge making, rather than in the specifics of the interactions/intra-actions I observed—just as Clarissa and I argue, in our coauthored study that the reliability of our collaborative case study is in both our collaborative methodology and in the heuristic we developed from our findings (Shivers-McNair and San Diego 2017). Similarly, in the study of the Rhetoric in the Making course I describe in Chapter 6, my coauthors and I offer both our collaborative methods and our recommendations for course design as opportunities for further user localization, rather than as generalizable truths (Shivers-McNair et al. 2018).

Still, even within the intended scope of this study and my findings, there are limitations. Emergence is at the heart of this study—emergence of a makerspace itself, of bodies and machines and objects, of the theoretical and methodological apparatus, of my relationship to makers and makerspaces, and of knowledge about making. But these many layers of emergence limit what I claim to know about developments in the spaces I studied. Even though the study is longitudinal and covers four years, I spent many months of the first year focused on orienting myself to an unfamiliar workspace (particularly its dynamic, permeable, fast-changing nature) and unfamiliar technologies, as well as building trust with the people in SoDo Makerspace. This had advantages: I empathized with others who identified as relatively new to the maker movement and could relate to the challenges of making oneself into a "maker." But a researcher and/or practitioner already familiar with the maker movement and/or already familiar with 3D fabrication technologies would likely have been able to observe and experience phenomena at a more fine-grained level than I was able to in the early months of my study.

Furthermore, my "low but steady level" of physical presence at the research site (Read 2011) had both advantages and limitations. On the one hand, it afforded a more longitudinal view of developments and helped me more clearly trace and construct genealogies of mattering over time, particularly since I was constructing and refining both the accounts themselves and the genealogical apparatus. On the other hand, because the composition and organization of people, machines, and objects in SoDo Makerspace can (and did) change so frequently in its four-year life span, a more intensive, day-to-day view could have illuminated more micro-level effects of these changes. Still, as I hope the stories in this book convey, the experiences and relationships that are the heart of this study have taught me much about making, about research, about rhetoric and writing, and about teaching.

These experience and relationships have also opened up many possible future directions for me: for example, I have envisioned a multisite comparative study of makerspaces. I can also envision an investigation of writing in a media-rich, adhocractic space that isn't necessarily a makerspace. And I can envision an examination of maker-inspired writing and rhetoric pedagogies. My decision to design an ethnographic case study of a makerspace was motivated by my belief that as rhetoric and writing studies grow more interested in makerspaces and the maker movement as potential pedagogical models, we need to understand the material-cultural phenomena we are importing. This matters particularly when there is a perception that the maker movement in the United States has not been "broadly successful at involving a diverse audience, especially over a sustained period of time," as Angela Calabrese Barton, Edna Tan, and Day Greenberg (2017) suggest (5).

But my understanding of issues of inclusion in the maker movement and of inclusion in the spaces I studied has also become more nuanced. As Candice Rai (2016) explains in her account of her practice of rhetorical ethnography:

> If I first entered the field with a type of critically edged project in mind that engaged in something of a left-leaning hermeneutics of suspicion, I exited it with the desire to perform something more akin to mapping the available means of persuasion as they circulated within complex and ambivalent contexts with as much empathy as possible. (26)

For example, Clarissa taught me to avoid starting with a blanket definition of "diversity" or "inclusion" (in the maker movement, and beyond) and to be willing to think expansively and contextually about the marking of differences. As I observed many times, she draws on her own definition of rhetoric as the "localization of information and processes for particular cultural and community contexts" to emphasize the importance of looking past the surface, finding ways to connect and reconnect, and taking time to understand each other as we negotiate and mark boundaries in acts of making.

The definitions of "making" and "maker" in and beyond the maker movement are certainly consequential—they privilege some bodies and traditions at the exclusion of other bodies and traditions. The consequences of these boundary marks are evident in scholarship on and accounts from the maker movement, and in the stories in this book. But I learned from Clarissa that it's possible to recognize and even work toward redressing the consequences of boundary marks while also dwelling in the nuances of working across difference in day-to-day interactions and relationships. By acknowledging the dynamic and complex nature of the marking of difference, we can attend to what Fatima El-Tayeb (2011) calls "fuzzy edges and intersections" (47–48). And as Clarissa reminds us, "Like the process of making, you never really get it right the first time. But the more we take the time to understand and allow ourselves and others to make mistakes, the better equipped we become to handle (or design) anything."

Clarissa's words apply not only to the ongoing work of negotiating and sustaining relationships, but also to my experience of the making of this book and to my understandings of possible futures for research on making. In addition to continuing to address and dwell in the nuances of issues of diversity and inclusion in the maker movement, I also envision continuing to look across and beyond makerspaces to understand and participate in the contemporary global phenomenon of the maker movement. My study offers a longitudinal examination of a makerspace working to establish itself in a city that is, in the words of one participant, a "graveyard" of relatively short-lived makerspaces. It also offers a longitudinal examination of a changing cohort of makerspace regulars as they face challenges of bringing their economic and social goals to fruition, and it offers a longitudinal examination of how makers are made (and unmade, and remade) in a makerspace.

A possible next step, then, is to examine multiple sites to begin to work toward an understanding of the similarities and nuances of the larger movement. As universities create their own makerspaces, it is worth comparing the kinds of making that matter in a university makerspace with the kinds of making that matter in a for-profit/public-benefit makerspace like SoDo Makerspace. It is also worth considering organizations like Makerologist that do not consider themselves makerspaces but do engage with the maker movement. It would also be worth further investigating similarities and differences in a for-profit/public-benefit makerspace with a nonprofit and/

or grant-funded makerspace, as education researchers like Kimberly M. Sheridan et al. (2014) model.

Furthermore, while scholars like human-computer interaction (HCI) researchers Sarah Fox, Rachel Rose Ulgado, and Daniela Rosner (2015) have investigated feminist hackerspaces (including the one in Seattle that closed in 2018), a sustained comparison of a feminist makerspace and a not-overtly-feminist makerspace could further elucidate issues of gender and inclusion in the movement. And while my own study has focused on a makerspace in the United States with English as its lingua franca, more studies of makerspaces in different countries and with different cultural and linguistic practices could contextualize knowledge of makerspaces and the maker movement beyond a US-centric perspective. Such work is modeled in the scholarship of HCI scholars like Silvia Lindtner, Shaowen Bardzell, and Jeffrey Bardzell (2016), who are engaged in ongoing research on maker communities in China and in Taiwan. Understanding similarities and differences across financial, institutional, geographic, linguistic, and cultural settings is important, whether the goal is to contribute to inter-disciplinary academic and practical knowledge about makerspaces and the maker movement or to make more informed choices about the pedagogical and technological practices we import from them into our classrooms, writing centers, libraries, and campuses.

As a researcher-teacher interested in preparing students to write in an economy increasingly comprised of media-rich "all-edge adhocracies" (Spinuzzi 2015), I envision further investigations of writing and making in and beyond the maker movement. For example, I envision that a study of the visibility and value of writing (and, of course, what and who count as writing and writers) could engage with points of communicative failures, with how people engage with writing on a day-to-day basis, and/or with the visibility of writing (particularly as opposed to other forms of making) in the space. The visibility of work matters immensely to its relative importance, and invisibility makes work matter less and become more difficult. My observations of SoDo Makerspace, in particular, suggest a similar issue with the visibility (and recognition) of writing and writers—particularly in Tony's case, but also in the case of the SoDo Makerspace blog (with its periods of activity and dormancy) and other social media, as well as various workflow tools (wikis, Trello, Slack, Google calendars, machine maintenance and repair manuals, instructional manuals, release forms and waivers, etc.). Ongoing investigation of the role of writing in maker communities could further enrich my understanding of how and why writing and writers are made more or less visible (or made to matter more or less). This, in turn, could inform how I teach writing, particularly to students whose occupational goals tend toward spaces where alphabetic communication both complements and competes with visual, aural, and 3D forms of communication.

Finally, an unexpected but welcome outcome of this project has been the emergence of a philosophy and practice of relational accountability that not only unifies various projects within my research agenda, but that also unifies my research and teaching in ways that I had not experienced before, in nearly a decade of teaching. In fact, the structure of this book—as it moves among and blends theory, methods, experiences, people, and pedagogies—is a microcosm of my lived experience during the study. The study and this book developed in response to and in the context of my research and teaching, and then reinfused itself into both my research and teaching. What I hope to carry forward is a relational approach to making that is both more than human and still human centered, inspired by Clarissa's use of the word *makerology* instead of *making*. On the Makerologist website, Clarissa defined makerology as "the area of study where science, technology, engineering, art, mathematics, and sociology intersect with the objective to produce something to benefit a network economy." Clarissa's definition centers both reflexivity (in the addition of *-ology*) and relationality (in the emphasis on benefiting a community). Such an approach can allow us to embrace the more than human possibilities of connections among humans and technologies while also centering humans, especially those who are marginalized by mainstream definitions and practices of making. This work—in and beyond the maker movement, in and beyond academia—begins with the relationships and communities that make making possible.

References

Agboka, Godwin Y. 2013. "Participatory Localization: A Social Justice Approach to Navigating Unenfranchised/Disenfranchised Cultural Sites." *Technical Communication Quarterly* 22(1): 28–49.

Ahmed, Sara. 2006. *Queer Phenomenology: Orientations, Objects, Others.* Durham: Duke University Press.

Alsup, Janet. 2010. "Beyond Member Checks: Moving toward Transformative Data Analysis." In *Change Matters: Critical Essays on Moving Social Justice Research from Theory to Policy*, edited by sj Miller and David E. Kirkland, 97–104. New York: Peter Lang.

Alvarez, Steven. 2019. "Rhetorical Autoethnography: Delinking English Language Learning in a Family Oral History." In *Rhetorics Elsewhere and Otherwise: Contested Modernities, Decolonial Visions*, edited by Romeo Garcia and Damián Baca, 85–111. Urbana: National Council of Teachers of English.

Arola, Kristin. 2018. "Composing as Culturing: An American Indian Approach to Digital Ethics." In *Handbook of Writing, Literacies, and Education in Digital Cultures*, edited by Kathy A. Mills, Amy Stornaiuolo, Anna Smith, and Jessica Zacher Pandya, 275–284. New York: Routledge.

Balsamo, Anne. 2011. *Designing Culture: The Technological Imagination at Work.* Durham: Duke University Press.

Banks, Adam. 2006. *Race, Rhetoric, and Technology: Searching for Higher Ground.* Urbana: National Council of Teachers of English.

Banks, Adam. 2011. *Digital Griots: African American Rhetoric in a Multimedia Age.* Carbondale: Southern Illinois University Press.

Barad, Karen. 2007. *Meeting the Universe Halfway: Quantum Physics and the Entanglement of Matter and Meaning.* Durham: Duke University Press.

Barad, Karen. 2012. "Nature's Queer Performativity." *Kvinder Køn og Forskning* 1–2: 25–54.

Barton, Angela Calabrese, Edna Tan, and Day Greenberg. 2017. "The Makerspace Movement: Sites of Possibilities for Equitable Opportunities to Engage Underrepresented Youth in STEM." *Teachers College Record* 119(7): 1–44.

Bawarshi, Anis. 2010. "The Challenges and Possibilities of Taking Up Multiple Discursive Resources in US College Composition." In *Cross-Language Relations in Composition*, edited by Bruce Horner, Min-Zhan Lu, and Paul Kei Matsuda, 196–203. Carbondale: Southern Illinois University Press.

Bay, Jennifer, Richard Johnson-Sheehan, and Devon Cook. 2018. "Design Thinking via Experiential Learning: Thinking like an Entrepreneur in Technical Communication Courses." *Programmatic Perspectives* 10(1): 172–200.

Blackley, Susan, Rachel Sheffield, Nicoleta Maynard, Rekha Koul, and Rebecca Walker. 2017. "'Makerspace' and Reflective Practice: Advancing Pre-service Teachers in STEM Education." *Australian Journal of Teacher Education* 42(3): 22–37.

Bratta, Phil, and Malea Powell. 2016. "Introduction to the Special Issue: Entering the Cultural Rhetorics Conversations." *enculturation* 21. http://enculturation.net/entering-the-cultural-rhetorics-conversations

Breuch, Lee-Ann Kastman. 2001. "The Overruled Dust Mite: Preparing Technical Communication Students to Interact with Clients." *Technical Communication Quarterly* 10(2): 193–210.

Bulmash, Greg. 2016. "Event Review: DevRel Summit." 14 August 2016. http://yiddish.ninja/event-review-devrel-summit/

Butler, Judith. 1993. *Bodies That Matter: On the Discursive Limits of "Sex."* New York: Routledge.

Cardinal, Alison. 2019. "Participatory Video: An Apparatus for Ethically Researching Literacy, Power, and Embodiment." *Computers and Composition* 53: 34–46.

Ceraso, Steph, Matthew Pavesich, and Jeremy Boggs (Designer). 2019. "Learning as Coordination: Postpedagogy and Design." *enculturation* 28. enculturation.net/learning_as_coordination.

Charlton, James I. 1998. *Nothing About Us without Us: Disability Oppression and Empowerment*. Berkeley: University of California Press.

Clark, J. Elizabeth. 2016. "From Selfies to Self-Representation in Electronically Mediated Reflection." In *A Rhetoric of Reflection*, edited by Kathleen B. Yancey, 149–165. Logan: Utah State University Press.

Clary-Lemon, Jennifer. 2019. "Gifts, Ancestors, and Relations: Notes toward an Indigenous New Materialism." *enculturation* 30. enculturation.net/gifts_ancestors_and_relations

Cobos, Casie, Gabriela Raquel Ríos, Donnie Johnson Sackey, Jennifer Sano-Franchini, and Angela M. Haas. 2018. "Interfacing Cultural Rhetorics: A History and a Call." *Rhetoric Review* 37(2): 139–154.

Cortez, José. 2017. "History." In *Decolonizing Rhetoric and Composition Studies: New Latinx Keywords for Theory and Pedagogy*, edited by Iris Ruiz and Raúl Sánchez, 49–62. New York: Palgrave Macmillan.

Costanza-Chock, Sasha. 2020. *Design Justice: Community-Led Practices to Build the Worlds We Need*. Cambridge: MIT Press.

Craig, Jacob. 2014. "Makers and Makerspaces: Teaching Composition in a Creative Economy." Pearson. http://unwrite.org/pearson/

Crenshaw, Kimberlé. 1989. "Demarginalizing the Intersection of Race and Sex: A Black Feminist Critique of Antidiscrimination Doctrine, Feminist Theory and Antiracist Politics." *University of Chicago Legal Forum* 1: 139–167.

Crowley, Sharon. 1999. "Afterword." In *Rhetorical Bodies*, edited by Jack Selzer and Sharon Crowley, 357–364. Madison: University of Wisconsin Press.

Cultural Rhetorics Theory Lab (Malea Powell, Daisy Levy, Andrea Riley Mukavetz, Marilee Brooks-Gillies, Maria Novotny, and Jennifer Fisch-Ferguson). 2014. "Our Story Begins Here: Constellating Cultural Rhetorics." *enculturation* 25. http://enculturation.net/our-story-begins-here

Cushman, Ellen. 2013. "Wampum, Sequoyan, and Story: Decolonizing the Digital Archive." *College English* 76(2): 115–135.

Del Hierro, Victor. 2018. "DJs, Playlists, and Community: Imagining Communication Design through Hip Hop." *Communication Design Quarterly* 7(2): 1–12. https://doi.org/10.1145/3358931.3358936

Doorley, Scott, and Scott Witthoft. 2012. *Make Space: How to Set the Stage for Creative Collaboration*. Hoboken: John Wiley & Sons.

Dougherty, Dale. 2019. "A Message from Dale and Team." *Make Community*. July 2019. https://help.make.co/hc/en-us/articles/203752459-Make-Community

El-Tayeb, Fatima. 2011. *European Others: Queering Ethnicity in Post-national Europe*. Minneapolis: University of Minnesota Press.

Eyman, Douglas. 2009. "Usability: Methodology and Design Practice for Writing Processes and Pedagogies." In *Rhetorically Rethinking Usability: Theories, Practices, and Methodologies*, edited by Susan K. Miller-Cochran and Rochelle L. Rodrigo, 213–228. New York: Hampton Press.

Faber, Brenton D. 2002. *Community Action and Organizational Change: Image, Narrative, and Identity*. Carbondale: Southern Illinois University Press.

Fernandes, Leela. 1997. *Producing Workers: The Politics of Gender, Class, and Culture in the Calcutta Jute Mills*. Philadelphia: University of Pennsylvania Press.

Fox, Sarah, Rachel Rose Ulgado, and Daniela K. Rosner. 2015. "Hacking Culture, Not Devices: Access and Recognition in Feminist Hackerspaces." In *Proceedings of the 15th ACM Conference on Computer Supported Cooperative Work and Social Computing*, Vancouver, BC, March 2015, 56–68. New York: ACM.

García, Romeo, and Damián Baca, eds. 2019. *Rhetorics Elsewhere and Otherwise: Contested Modernities, Decolonial Visions*. Urbana: National Council of Teachers of English.

George, Diana. 2002. "From Analysis to Design: Visual Communication in the Teaching of Writing." *College Composition and Communication* 54(1): 11–39.

Gollihue, Krystin N. 2019. "Re-making the Makerspace: Bodies, Power, and Identity in Critical Making Practices." PhD diss., North Carolina State University.

Gonzales, Laura. 2018a. *Sites of Translation: What We Can Learn from Multilinguals about Writing, Rhetoric, and Technology*. Ann Arbor: University of Michigan Press.

Gonzales, Laura. 2018b. "Designing for Intersectional, Interdependent Accessibility: A Case Study of Multilingual Technical Content." *Communication Design Quarterly* 6(4): 34–45.

Grabill, Jeffrey. 2013. "On Being Useful: Rhetoric and the Work of Engagement." In *The Public Work of Rhetoric*, edited by David Coogan. Columbia: University of South Carolina Press.

Guerra, Juan C. 2013. "Cultivating Transcultural Citizenship in a Discursive Democracy." In *Texts of Consequence: Composing Rhetorics of Social Activism for the Writing Classroom*, edited by Christopher Wilkey and Nicholas Mauriello, 83–115. New York: Hampton Press.

Haas, Angela M. 2007. "Wampum as Hypertext: An American Indian Intellectual Tradition of Multimedia Theory and Practice." *Studies in American Indian Literatures* 19(4): 77–100.

Haas, Angela M. 2012. "Race, Rhetoric, and Technology: A Case Study of Decolonial Technical Communication Theory, Methodology, and Pedagogy." *Journal of Business and Technical Communication* 26(3): 277–310.

Hackster.io. 2016. *Hackster.io Maker Survey*. https://www.hackster.io/survey

Hagel, John, John Seely Brown, and Duleesha Kulasooriya. 2013. *A Movement in the Making*. London: Deloitte University Press.

Hammersley, Martin. 2011. *Methodology: Who Needs It?* Los Angeles: Sage Publications.

Haraway, Donna. 1988. "Situated Knowledges: The Science Question in Feminism and the Privilege of Partial Perspective." *Feminist Studies* 14(3): 575–599.

Haraway, Donna. 1991. *Simians, Cyborgs, and Women: The Re-invention of Nature*. London: Routledge.

Harris, Joseph. 2012. *A Teaching Subject: Composition since 1966*. Logan: Utah State University Press.

Hatcher, Jessamyn, and Thuy Linh Nguyen Tu. 2017. "'Make What You Love': Homework, the Handmade, and the Precarity of the Maker Movement." *Women's Studies Quarterly* 45(3–4): 271–286.

Hawisher, Gail, and Cynthia Selfe, with Brittney Moraski and Melissa Pearson. 2004. "Becoming Literate in the Information Age: Cultural Ecologies and the Literacies of Technology." *College Composition and Communication* 55(4): 642–692.

Ingold, Tim. 2013. *Making: Anthropology, Archaeology, Art and Architecture*. New York: Routledge.

Johnson, Robert R. 1998. *User-Centered Technology: A Rhetorical Theory for Computers and Other Mundane Artifacts*. Albany: State University of New York Press.

Jones, Natasha N. 2016. "Narrative Inquiry in Human-Centered Design: Examining Silence and Voice to Promote Social Justice in Design Scenarios." *Journal of Technical Writing and Communication* 46(4): 471–492.

Jones, Natasha N., Kristen R. Moore, and Rebecca Walton. 2016. "Disrupting the Past to Disrupt the Future: An Antenarrative of Technical Communication." *Technical Communication Quarterly* 25(4): 211–229.

Jones, Natasha N., and Rebecca Walton. 2018. "Using Narratives to Foster Critical Thinking about Diversity and Social Justice." In *Key Theoretical Frameworks: Teaching Technical Communication in the Twenty-First Century*, edited by Angela M. Haas and Michelle Eble, 241–267. Logan: Utah State University Press.

Jung, Julie. 2014. "Systems Rhetoric: A Dynamic Coupling of Explanation and Description." *enculturation* 17. http://enculturation.net/systems-rhetoric

Jung, Julie, and Kellie Sharp-Hoskins. 2017. "Emergent Mattering: Building Rhetorical Ethics at the Limits of the Human." In *Kenneth Burke + the Posthuman*, edited by Chris Mays, Nathaniel A. Rivers, and Kellie Sharp-Hoskins. University Park: Pennsylvania State University Press.

Lauer, Claire, and Eva Brumberger. 2016. "Technical Communication as User Experience in a Broadening Industry Landscape." *Technical Communication* 63: 248–264.

Laurier, Eric. 2014. "Capturing Motion: Video Set-ups for Driving, Cycling and Walking." In *The Routledge Handbook of Mobilities*, edited by Peter Adey, David Bissell, Kevin Hannam, Peter Merriman, and Mimi Sheller, 493–502. London: Taylor and Francis.

Law, John. 2002. *Aircraft Stories: Decentering the Object in Technoscience.* Durham: Duke University Press.

Leverenz, Carrie. 2014. "Design Thinking and the Wicked Problem of Teaching Writing." *Computers and Composition* 33: 1–12.

Levine, Faythe, and Courtney Heimerl. 2008. *Handmade Nation: The Rise of DIY, Art, Craft, and Design.* New York: Princeton Architectural Press.

Licona, Adela C., and Karma R. Chávez. 2015. "Relational Literacies and Their Coalitional Possibilities." *Peitho.* http://peitho.cwshrc.org/relational-literacies-and-their-coalitional-possibilities-2/

Lindtner, Silvia, Shaowen Bardzell, and Jeffrey Bardzell. 2016. "Reconstituting the Utopian Vision of Making: HCI after Technosolutionism." In *Proceedings of the 2016 CHI Conference on Human Factors in Computing Systems*, San Jose, CA, May 2016, 1390–1402. New York: ACM.

Lindtner, Silvia, and David Li. 2012. "Created in China: The Makings of China's Hackerspace Community." *Interactions* 19(6): 18–22.

Livingston, Violet A. 2015. "The Queer Art & Rhetoric of Consent: Theories, Practices, Pedagogies." PhD diss., Michigan State University.

Long, Elenore. 2014. "Engaging Public Administrators in Training: Technical Communication as a Responsive Rhetorical Art." *2014 IEEE International Professional Communication Conference (IPCC)*, Pittsburgh, PA, October 2015. IEEE Xplore.

Losse, Kate. 2016. "The Art of Failing Upward." *New York Times.* 5 March 2016. https://www.nytimes.com/2016/03/06/opinion/sunday/the-art-of-failing-upward.html

Lynch, Paul. 2013. *After Pedagogy: The Experience of Teaching.* Urbana: National Council of Teachers of English.

Maker Media. 2013. *Makerspace Playbook.* https://makered.org/wp-content/uploads/2014/09/Makerspace-Playbook-Feb-2013.pdf

Maker Media. 2015. Fact Sheet. http://makermedia.com/press/fact-sheet/

Maker Media. 2017. "Maker Faire Bay Area Celebrates a Dozen Years as the Maker Movement Continues to Engage & Inspire." Maker Faire Press Release. 8 June 2017. https://www.prnewswire.com/news-releases/maker-faire-bay-area-celebrates-a-dozen-years-as-the-maker-movement-continues-to-engage—inspire-300471098.html?tc=eml_cleartime

Marback, Richard. 2008. "Unclenching the Fist: Embodying Rhetoric and Giving Objects Their Due." *Rhetoric Society Quarterly* 38(1): 46–65.

Marback, Richard. 2009. "Embracing Wicked Problems: The Turn to Design in Composition Studies." *College Composition and Communication* 61(2): 397–419.

McNely, Brian, Clay Spinuzzi, and Christa Teston. 2015. "Contemporary Research Methodologies in Technical Communication." *Technical Communication Quarterly* 24(1): 1–13.

McPherson, Tara. 2018. *Feminist in a Software Lab: Difference + Design.* Cambridge: Harvard University Press.

Melo, Marijel (Maggie) M. 2018. "The Shadow Rhetorics of Innovation: Maker Culture, Gender, and Technology." PhD diss., University of Arizona.

Mignolo, Walter D. 2007. "Delinking: The Rhetoric of Modernity, the Logic of Coloniality and the Grammar of De-coloniality." *Cultural Studies* 21(2–3): 449–514.

Miner, Dylan A. T. 2019. "*Mawadisidiwag miinawaa wiidanokiindiwag* // They visit and work together." In *Makers, Crafters, Educators: Working for Cultural Change*, edited by Elizabeth Garber, Lisa Hochtritt, and Manisha Sharma, 131–134. New York: Routledge.

Mukavetz, Andrea Riley. 2018. "Decolonial Theory and Methodology." *Composition Studies* 46(1): 124–140.

Murray, Sarah, and Megan Sapnar Ankerson. 2016. "Lez Takes Time: Designing Lesbian Contact in Geosocial Networking Apps." *Critical Studies in Media Communication* 33(1): 53–69.

Myers, Kelly A. 2016. "Metanoic Movement: The Transformative Power of Regret." *College Composition and Communication* 67(3): 385–410.

Nowacek, Rebecca S. 2011. *Agents of Integration: Understanding Transfer as a Rhetorical Act*. Carbondale: Southern Illinois University Press.

Palmeri, Jason. 2012. *Remixing Composition: A History of Multimodal Writing Pedagogy*. Carbondale: Southern Illinois University Press.

Paradis, James. 1991. "Text and Action: The Operator's Manual in Context and in Court." In *Textual Dynamics of the Professions: Historical and Contemporary Studies of Writing in Professional Communities*, edited by Charles Bazerman and James Paradis, 256–278. Madison: University of Wisconsin Press.

Patel, Leigh. 2015. *Decolonizing Education Research: From Ownership to Answerability*. New York: Routledge.

Patel, Lisa (Leigh). 2014. "Countering Coloniality in Educational Research: From Ownership to Answerability." *Educational Studies* 50(4): 357–377.

Pflugfelder, Ehren H. 2015. "Rhetoric's New Materialism: From Micro-rhetoric to Microbrew." *Rhetoric Society Quarterly* 45(5): 441–461.

Pink, Sarah. 2015. *Doing Sensory Ethnography*. Thousand Oaks: Sage Publications.

Powell, Malea. 2012. "2012 CCCC Chair's Address: Stories Take Place—a Performance in One Act." *College Composition and Communication* 64(2): 383–406.

Price, Margaret. 2011. *Mad at School: Rhetorics of Mental Disability and Academic Life*. Ann Arbor: University of Michigan Press.

Price, Margaret, and Stephanie Kerschbaum. 2016. "Stories of Methodology: Interviewing Sideways, Crooked and Crip." *Canadian Journal of Disability Studies* 5(3). https://doi.org/10.15353/cjds.v5i3.295

Purdy, James. 2014. "What Can Design Thinking Offer Writing Studies?" *College Composition and Communication* 65(4): 612–641.

Rai, Candice S. 2016. *Democracy's Lot: Rhetoric, Publics, and the Places of Invention*. Tuscaloosa: University of Alabama Press.

Ratcliffe, Krista. 2005. *Rhetorical Listening: Identification, Gender, Whiteness*. Carbondale: Southern Illinois University Press.

Ratto, Matt. 2011. "Critical Making: Conceptual and Material Studies in Technology and Social Life. *Information Society* 27(4): 252–260.

Read, Sarah. 2011. "Network Rhetoric: A Network Ethnography of the Knowledge

Work of System Builders in Child Care and Early Learning." PhD diss., University of Washington.

Rhodes, Jacqueline, and Jonathan Alexander. 2015. *Techne: Queer Meditations on Writing the Self.* Logan: Utah State University Press. https://ccdigitalpress.org/techne

Ríos, Gabriela Raquel. 2015. "Cultivating Land-Based Literacies and Rhetorics." *Literacy in Composition Studies* 3(1): 60–70.

Rittel, Horst W., and Melvin M. Webber. 1974. "Wicked Problems." *Man-Made Futures* 26(1): 272–280.

Rose, Emma J., Robert Racadio, Kalen Wong, Shally Nguyen, Jee Kim, and Abbie Zahler. 2017. "Community-Based User Experience: Evaluating the Usability of Health Insurance Information with Immigrant Patients." *IEEE Transactions on Professional Communication* 60(2): 214–231.

Ross, Derek. 2013. "Deep Audience Analysis: A Proposed Method for Analyzing Audiences for Environment-Related Communication." *Technical Communication* 60: 94–117.

Royster, Jacqueline Jones, and Gesa Kirsch. 2012. *Feminist Rhetorical Practices: New Horizons for Rhetoric, Composition, and Literacy Studies.* Carbondale: Southern Illinois University Press.

Sackey, Donnie Johnson. 2018. "An Environmental Justice Paradigm for Technical Communication." In *Key Theoretical Frameworks: Teaching Technical Communication in the Twenty-First Century*, edited by Angela M. Haas and Michelle Eble, 138–160. Logan: Utah State University Press.

Sánchez, Raúl. 2017a. *Inside the Subject: A Theory of Identity for the Study of Writing.* Urbana: National Council of Teachers of English.

Sánchez, Raúl. 2017b. "Writing." In *Decolonizing Rhetoric and Composition Studies: New Latinx Keywords for Theory and Pedagogy*, edited by Iris Ruiz and Raúl Sánchez, 77–90. New York: Palgrave Macmillan.

Sandoval, Chela. 2000. *Methodology of the Oppressed.* Minneapolis: University of Minnesota Press.

Sano-Franchini, Jennifer. 2015. "Cultural Rhetorics and the Digital Humanities: Toward Cultural Reflexivity in Digital Making." In *Rhetoric and the Digital Humanities*, edited by Jim Ridolfo and William Hart-Davidson, 49–64. Chicago: University of Chicago Press.

Santos, Mark C., and Megan M. McIntyre. 2016. "Toward a Technical Communication Made Whole: Disequilibrium, Creativity, and Postpedagogy." *Composition Forum* 33. http://compositionforum.com/issue/33/techcomm.php

Sayers, Jentery, ed. 2017. *Making Things and Drawing Boundaries: Experiments in the Digital Humanities.* Minneapolis: University of Minnesota Press.

Schultz, Tristan, Danah Abdulla, Ahmed Ansari, Ece Canlı, Mahmoud Keshavarz, Matthew Kiem, Luiza Prado de O. Martins, and Pedro J. S. Vieira de Oliveira. 2018. "What Is at Stake with Decolonizing Design? A Roundtable." *Design and Culture* 10(1): 81–101.

Selfe, Cynthia. 2009. "The Movement of Air, the Breath of Meaning: Aurality and Multimodal Composing." *College Composition and Communication* 60(4): 616–663.

Selfe, Cynthia, and Richard Selfe. 1994. "The Politics of the Interface: Power and Its Exercise in Electronic Contact Zones." *College Composition and Communication* 45(4): 480–504.

Seo, Joo Young, and Gabriela Richard. 2018. "Accessibility, Making and Tactile Robotics: Facilitating Collaborative Learning and Computational Thinking for Learners with Visual Impairments." Poster presentation, International Society of the Learning Sciences, London, 2018.

Sherrill, John. 2014. "Makers: Technical Communication in Post-industrial Participatory Communities." Master's thesis, Purdue University.

Sheridan, David. 2010. "Fabricating Consent: Three-Dimensional Objects as Rhetorical Compositions." *Computers and Composition* 27: 249–265.

Sheridan, Kimberly M., Erica Rosenfeld Halverson, Breanne Litts, Lisa Brahms, Lynette Jacobs-Priebe, and Trevor Owens. 2014. "Learning in the Making: A Comparative Case Study of Three Makerspaces." *Harvard Educational Review* 84(4): 505–531.

Shipka, Jody. 2011. *Toward a Composition Made Whole*. Pittsburgh: University of Pittsburgh Press.

Shipka, Jody. 2016. "Transmodality in/and Processes of Making: Changing Dispositions and Practice." *College English* 78(3): 250–257.

Shivers-McNair, Ann. 2017. "3D Interviewing with Researcher POV Video: Bodies and Knowledge in the Making." *Kairos* 21(2). http://praxis.technorhetoric.net/tiki-index.php?page=PraxisWiki%3A_%3A3D+Interviewing

Shivers-McNair, Ann. 2019. "Making Knowledge: A Kit for Researching 3D Rhetorics." *enculturation* 29. http://enculturation.net/3D_rhetorics

Shivers-McNair, Ann, Joy Phillips, Alyse Campbell, Hanh H. Mai, Alice Yan, John F. Macy, James Wenlock, Savannah Fry, and Yishan Guan. 2018. "User-Centered Design in and beyond the Classroom: Toward an Accountable Practice." *Computers and Composition* 49: 36–47.

Shivers-McNair, Ann, and Clarissa San Diego. 2017. "Localizing Communities, Goals, Communication, and Inclusion: A Collaborative Approach." *Technical Communication* 64(2): 97–112.

Sirc, Geoffrey. 2003. *English Composition as a Happening*. Logan: Utah State University Press.

Slattery, Shaun. 2005. "Technical Writing as Textual Coordination: An Argument for the Value of Writers' Skills with Information Technology." *Technical Communication* 52(3): 353–360.

Smith, Linda Tuhiwai. 2013. *Decolonizing Methodologies: Research and Indigenous Peoples*. London: Zed Books.

Spinuzzi, Clay. 2015. *All Edge: Inside the New Workplace Networks*. Chicago: University of Chicago Press.

Steele, Katherine M., Maya Cakmak, and Brianna Blaser. 2018. "Accessible Making: Designing Makerspaces for Accessibility." *International Journal of Designs for Learning* 9(1): 114–121.

Stevens, Sharon McKenzie. 2004. "Debating Ecology: Ethnographic Writing That 'Makes a Difference.'" In *Ethnography Unbound: From Theory Shock to Critical Praxis*, edited by Stephen Gilbert Brown and Sidney I. Dobrin, 157–180. Albany: State University of New York Press.

Suchman, Lucy. 2002. "Located Accountabilities in Technology Production." *Scandinavian Journal of Information Systems* 14(2): 91–105.

Sun, Huatong. 2012. *Cross-Cultural Technology Design: Creating Culture-Sensitive Technology for Local Users*. New York: Oxford University Press.

Takayoshi, Pamela, Emily Huot, and Megan Huot. 1999. "No Boys Allowed: The World Wide Web as a Clubhouse for Girls." *Computers and Composition* 16: 89–106.

Tham, Jason C. K. 2019. "Multimodality, Makerspaces, and the Making of a Maker Pedagogy for Technical Communication and Rhetoric." PhD diss., University of Minnesota.

Tuck, Eve, and K. Wayne Yang. 2012. "Decolonization Is Not a Metaphor." *Decolonization* 1(1): 1–40.

Vertesi, Janet. 2015. *Seeing Like a Rover: How Robots, Teams, and Images Craft Knowledge of Mars*. Chicago: University of Chicago Press.

Vossoughi, Shirin, Paula K. Hooper, and Meg Escudé. 2016. "Making through the Lens of Culture and Power: Toward Transformative Visions for Educational Equity." *Harvard Educational Review* 86(2): 206–232.

Walton, Rebecca. 2016. "Supporting Human Dignity and Human Rights: A Call to Adopt the First Principle of Human-Centered Design." *Journal of Technical Writing and Communication* 46(4): 402–426.

Walton, Rebecca, Kristen R. Moore, and Natasha N. Jones. 2019. *Technical Communication after the Social Justice Turn*. New York: Routledge.

Walton, Rebecca, Maggie Zraly, and Jean Pierre Mugengana. 2015. "Values and Validity: Navigating Messiness in a Community-Based Research Project." *Technical Communication Quarterly* 24(1): 45–69.

West-Puckett, Stephanie J. 2017. "Materializing Makerspaces: Queerly Composing Space, Time, and (What) Matters." PhD diss., East Carolina University.

Wilson, Shawn. 2008. *Research Is Ceremony: Indigenous Research Methods*. Black Point: Fernwood Publishing.

Womack, Anne-Marie, Annelise Blanchard, Cassie Wang, and Mary Catherine Jessee. n.d. *Accessible Syllabus*. Accessed 18 Aug. 2020. https://www.accessiblesyllabus.com/.

Woods, Dan. 2017. "TechShop Closes Doors, Files Bankruptcy." *Make: Magazine*. 15 November 2017. https://makezine.com/2017/11/15/techshop-closes-doors-files-bankruptcy/

Wysocki, Anne Frances. 2012. "Introduction: Into Between—On Composition in Mediation." In *Composing (Media) = Composing (Embodiment)*, edited by Kristin Arola and Anne Frances Wysocki, 1–22. Logan: Utah State University Press.

Wysocki, Anne Frances, and Johndan Johnson-Eilola. 1999. "Blinded by the Letter: Why Are We Using Literacy as a Metaphor for Everything Else?" In *Passions, Pedagogies, and 21st Century Technologies*, edited by Cynthia Selfe and Gail Hawisher, 349–368. Logan: Utah State University Press.

Yancey, Kathleen B., ed. 2016. *A Rhetoric of Reflection*. Logan: Utah State University Press.

Yergeau, M. Remi. 2017. *Authoring Autism: On Rhetoric and Neurological Queerness*. Durham: Duke University Press.

Index

Printed and bound by CPI Group (UK) Ltd, Croydon, CR0 4YY

09/06/2025

14685674-0004